NAzik

LIFE ON EARTH
BEFORE LIFE

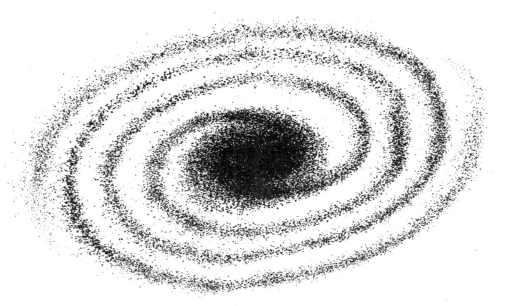

THE DIAGRAM GROUP

Facts On File, Inc.

Life On Earth: Before Life

Written, edited, and produced by Diagram Visual Information Ltd

Editorial director:	Denis Kennedy
Editors:	Bender Richardson White, Gordon Lee
Contributor:	Gerard E. Cheshire
Indexer:	Martin Hargreaves
Art director:	Roger Kohn
Senior designer:	Lee Lawrence
Designers:	Anthony Atherton, Christian Owens
Illustrators:	Pavel Kostal, Kathleen McDougall, Coral Mula, Graham Rosewarne
Picture researcher:	Neil McKenna

Facts On File, Inc.
132 West 31st Street
New York NY 10001

For Library of Congress Cataloging-in-Publication Data, please contact Facts On File, Inc.
ISBN 0-8160-5045-7

Facts On File books are available at special discounts when purchased in bulk quantities for businesses, associations, institutions, or sales promotions. Please call our Special Sales Department in New York at 212/967-8800 or 800/322-8755.

You can find Facts On File on the World Wide Web at: http://www.factsonfile.com

Printed in the United States of America

EB Diagram   10   9   8   7   6   5   4   3   2   1

This book is printed on acid-free paper.

Contents

THIS BOOK is a concise, illustrated guide to the formation of the universe, the solar system, the Earth, and to the geology and geography of our planet. The story has taken hundreds of millions of years, and is one that continues today. Texts, explanatory diagrams, illustrations, captions, and feature boxes combine to help readers grasp important information. A glossary clarifies the more difficult scientific terms for younger students, while a list of websites provides links to other relevant sources of additional information.

Chapter 1, *Universal Origin*, deals with the way in which scientists think the universe started, and the evidence for the dominating theories.

Chapter 2, *Universal Structure*, covers the formation and development of galaxies, stars, and other cosmic objects.

Chapter 3, *Our Solar System*, explains the formation, structure, and mechanics of our familiar part of the cosmos—from the Sun, a typical star, to the planets and their moons, asteroids, and meteorites.

Chapter 4, *Planet Earth*, is a concise description of the Earth as a cosmic object orbiting a star, of the Moon as an accompanying satellite, and of the formation and properties of the chemicals found on Earth.

Chapter 5, *Tectonic Movements*, looks at the structure and forces within the Earth's core and crust that have formed, and still shape the features of the ocean floor and the continental landmasses.

Chapter 6, *Rocks*, examines the different minerals and compounds that make up the strata, or layers, of the Earth's crust.

Chapter 7, *Erosion and Other Processes*, scrutinizes the natural mechanisms by which rocks are worn down by the weather to form the landscape we see around us today. It also explains such global changes as tides, currents, the seasons, climate, and the first appearance of life on Earth.

Before Life is one of six titles in the Life On Earth series that looks at the evolution and diversity of our planet, its characteristic features, and the living things that used to, or now, inhabit it.

The series features all life-forms, from bacteria and algae to trees and mammals. It also highlights the infinite variety of adaptations and strategies for survival among living things, and describes different habitats, how they evolved, and the communities of creatures that inhabit them. Individual chapters discuss the characteristics of specific taxonomic groups of living things, or types of landscape, or planetary features.

Life On Earth has been written by natural history experts and is generously illustrated with line drawings, labeled diagrams, and maps. The series provides students with a solid, necessary foundation for their future studies in science.

Most religions over the world have their own stories suggesting how the universe began. All of these stories are described as "creationist beliefs" because they typically involve a god, or gods, who created everything by divine power.

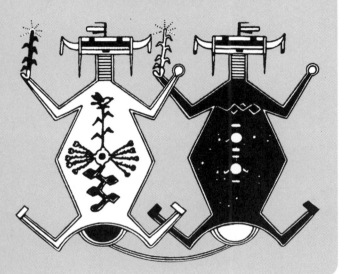

CREATIONIST BELIEFS emanate from a time in human history before science could offer alternative explanations of the world. They persist today among the religious, partly because of indoctrination, but also because belief in spiritual explanations for existence seems to fulfill a fundamental need in the human mind.

Scientists do not operate on a belief system, but instead use one of "secular ideas." Scientists investigate their secular ideas by formulating hypotheses and theories based on observation and reasoning. Having done so, they search for empirical proof or evidence to back up their ideas.

The best scientific practice is to attempt complete impartiality throughout the course of the investigative process, without allowing beliefs or opinions to enter the equation.

The universe
It is vast, and it may even be infinite. It is impossible to know why, or how, it exists.

IT'S A FACT
Having gathered their evidence, scientists reach conclusions about the accuracy of their original ideas, and make adjustments to their hypotheses and theories accordingly. Scientific investigation is an ongoing process, where scientists remain open-minded and ready to adapt their ideas for the sake of pursuing the truth. In this way, science has systematically proposed and modified its ideas on the origin and nature of the universe.

1 *Observation* 〉〉 **2** *Reasoning* 〉〉 **3** *Hypothesis* 〉〉 **4** *Experiment* 〉〉 **5** *Conclusion* 〉〉 **6** *Theory*

© DIAGRAM

In 1920, U.S. astronomer Vesto Slipher discovered that the universe was expanding by observing the distortion of light waves from distant galaxies. In 1923, Edwin Hubble suggested that the universe might be thought of as a balloon being steadily inflated.

The "big bang theory"
According to this theory, space, time, energy, and matter were all created, in one huge explosion, about 15 billion years ago.

THE DISCOVERIES made by Vesto Slipher and Edwin Hubble in the 1920s implied that the universe must have begun from a single point in time and space. Modern cosmology was thus born as scientists began postulating theories to explain the origin of the universe. In 1927 the "big bang theory," in which the universe began with the explosion of an extremely dense ball of matter, was proposed by Belgian astrophysicist George Lemaitre.

In 1948, three British astronomers, Herman Bondi, Thomas Gold, and Fred Hoyle, proposed a radically different solution: the "steady state theory." They suggested that the universe perpetually generates new matter to fill the void left by receding galaxies. It conveniently avoided the need for a beginning of time and space, but required that the

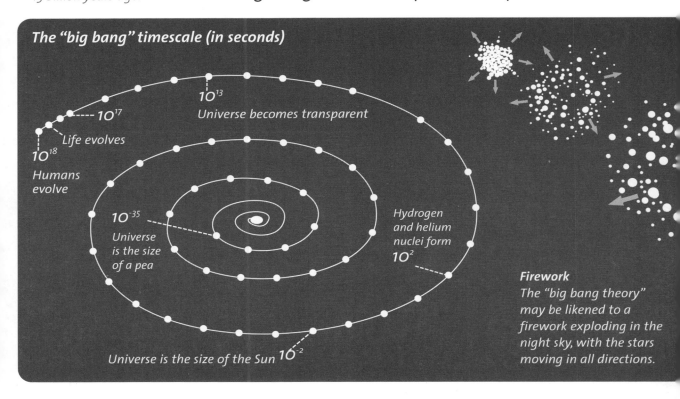

The "big bang" timescale (in seconds)

10^{13}
Universe becomes transparent

10^{17}
Life evolves

10^{18}
Humans evolve

10^{-35}
Universe is the size of a pea

Hydrogen and helium nuclei form
10^2

Universe is the size of the Sun 10^{-2}

Firework
The "big bang theory" may be likened to a firework exploding in the night sky, with the stars moving in all directions.

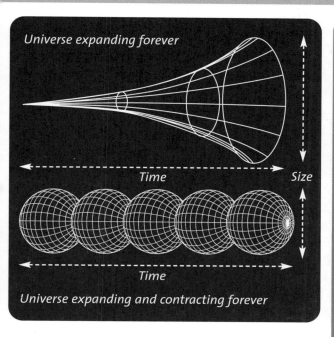

Universe expanding forever

Time

Size

Time

Universe expanding and contracting forever

IT'S A FACT
Slipher's and Hubble's theories remained equally popular until 1964 when U.S. physicist Robert Dicke predicted the existence of "cosmic microwave background radiation" to support the big bang theory. U.S. radio astronomers, Arno Penzias and Robert Wilson, duly discovered this to be the case in 1965, and so the steady state theory fell from favor. Dicke favored a compromise theory—the "cyclical evolutionary theory"—in which the universe repeatedly expands and contracts over phases of about 45 billion years.

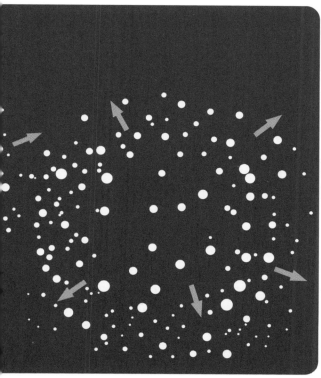

universe be infinite. It had earlier been suggested that, if the universe were infinite, then space must be uniformly white instead of black because everywhere would be filled with the light from an infinite number of stars. However, in 1929, Edwin Hubble had discovered the so-called "Hubble's law," which showed that any galaxies more than 10 billion light years from Earth must vanish from view. This is simply because they are receding at a speed greater than the speed of light, so that the light emitted by their stars can never reach us. Hubble's law showed that there was a divide between the observable and unobservable universe, so that it may or may not be infinite.

Theories on the origin of the universe rely on scientific evidence. For example, we know that the universe is expanding because of the distortion in light waves from distant galaxies.

Christian Johann Doppler   Edwin Hubble

The "Doppler effect"
This is the term used when white light waves appear to be reddish when they are traveling away from the Earth.

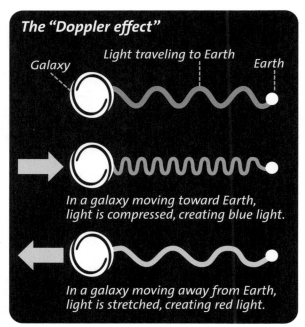

The "Doppler effect"

Galaxy
Light traveling to Earth
Earth

In a galaxy moving toward Earth, light is compressed, creating blue light.

In a galaxy moving away from Earth, light is stretched, creating red light.

DISTORTION in light waves from distant galaxies is known as "red shift." White light, such as that from our Sun, reaches us at the speed of light. However, if the source of light is traveling away from us, the light waves become stretched so that the light is seen to shift to the red end of its spectrum. Conversely, if a galaxy were traveling toward us, the light would be seen to shift toward the blue end of its spectrum ("blue shift") due to the compression of light waves. These distortions, known as the "Doppler effect," were first observed in sound waves by Austrian physicist Christian Johann Doppler in 1842.

The "red shift" phenomenon enabled Edwin Hubble to formulate a law which calculates the relationship between the distance of galaxies from the Earth and their speed of recession from the Earth. It is always the same and is thus known as "Hubble's constant." This allowed science to calculate the approximate age and size of the universe simply by comparing the degree of "red shift" throughout the

IT'S A FACT

"Microwave background" is the abbreviation for "cosmic microwave background radiation," used by Robert Dicke in 1964 to reinforce the "big bang theory." It is a weak, but uniform, field of electromagnetic radiation detectable throughout the sky, and is considered to be evidence of the initial explosion. The idea is that the microwave background field has filled the space occupied by the universe. As the universe has expanded, so the wavelength of the microwave background has lengthened to fill the space. It currently has a wavelength of about 0.04 inches (1 mm).

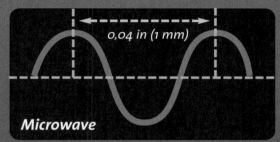

0.04 in (1 mm)

Microwave

galaxies within the observable universe. "Hubble's constant" relies, however, on the assumption that there is no deceleration of the universe's expansion. This is refuted by cyclical evolutionary theorists, as they hold that the universe expands and contracts over and over again. In fact, recent evidence suggests that the universe's current rate of expansion is actually accelerating, which confuses matters still further.

"Hubble time" (below)
Edwin Hubble calculated that the universe is about 20 billion years old.

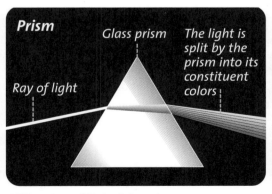

Prism

Glass prism

The light is split by the prism into its constituent colors

Ray of light

Diffraction of light (above)
White light is diffracted, or broken apart, into a spectrum of wavelengths by the prism.

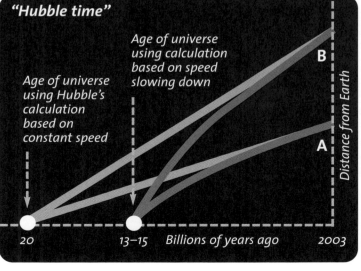

"Hubble time"

Age of universe using calculation based on speed slowing down

B

Age of universe using Hubble's calculation based on constant speed

A

Distance from Earth

20   13–15   *Billions of years ago*   2003

© DIAGRAM

Assuming the universe to be finite, as most scientists do, it is still inconceivably large. It comprises hundreds of millions of galaxies traveling away from one another. Some galaxies are isolated, while others are in clusters of thousands.

THERE ARE THREE FUNDAMENTAL TYPES of galaxy: elliptical, spiral, and barred spiral. Galaxies are large, rotating clouds of stars, and it is thought that elliptical galaxies give rise to the other forms as their rotation causes arms to spiral away from the central core. Intermediate galaxies are known as lenticular galaxies. Our own galaxy is called the Milky Way and is a spiral galaxy containing 100 billion stars. It is about 100,000 light-years in diameter and some 20,000 light-years from top to bottom. The Sun orbits the center of the Milky Way once every 220 million years, and is positioned roughly 30,000 light-years away from it.

To give some idea of the scale of our galaxy alone, the nearest star to the Sun is a faint red dwarf called *Proxima*

Types of galaxy

Elliptical

Spiral

Barred spiral

Galaxies (above)
The geometric shapes of galaxies are normally dictated by rotational forces.

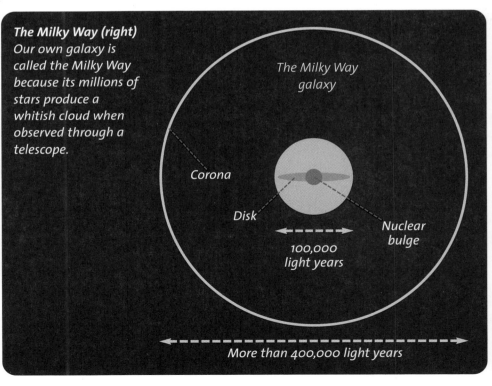

The Milky Way (right)
Our own galaxy is called the Milky Way because its millions of stars produce a whitish cloud when observed through a telescope.

The Milky Way galaxy

Corona

Disk

Nuclear bulge

100,000 light years

More than 400,000 light years

Centauri, which is 4.24 light-years away. A single light-year is the distance light will travel through space in one year, which is approximately 5,880 billion miles (9,408 billion km). So *Proxima Centauri* is about 25,000 billion miles (40 billion km) from us. Yet the distance between the Earth and *Proxima Centauri* is negligible in cosmological terms, for the universe itself is estimated to be at least 10 billion light-years in diameter. That works out at a distance of 58.8 billion trillion miles (94.6 billion trillion km) across.

STRANGE BUT TRUE

Whether the universe is perceived to be infinite or finite depends on one's point of view with regard to scientific theories. People tend to choose a preference according to whether they feel more comfortable with the idea that space and time have no beginning or end, or the idea that they both started at a particular point. Either way, such concepts test the very limits of human imagination and logical thought.

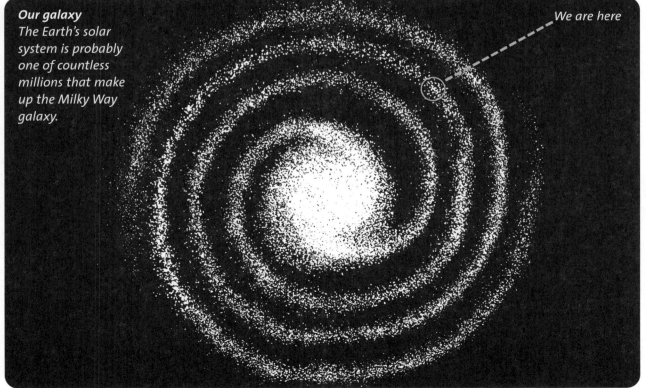

Our galaxy
The Earth's solar system is probably one of countless millions that make up the Milky Way galaxy.

We are here

© DIAGRAM

The forces responsible for the formation of stars are rotation, centrifugal, and centripetal forces.

STARS BEGIN THEIR LIVES as clouds of interstellar gas and dust called nebulae. A nebula condenses until it becomes a spinning mass of matter in space. The rotation provides centrifugal force, while gravitation provides centripetal force, so that the star ultimately stabilizes according to the amount of matter available, and its rate of revolution. Given sufficient mass, a star will initiate nuclear reactions and begin emitting energy in the form of solar radiation as its atoms collide with one another under compression.

Centrifugal force is the force that makes an object want to move away from the center of its point of rotation. Centripetal force is the opposite, but is not generated by movement. Instead, it

Centrifugal forces

Centripetal forces

Opposed forces
Centrifugal and centripetal forces become locked in perpetual motion.

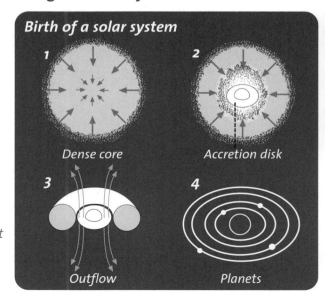

Birth of a solar system

1
Dense core

2
Accretion disk

3
Outflow

4
Planets

Birth of a solar system
Rotation and gravitation provide the centrifugal and centripetal forces that create solar systems.

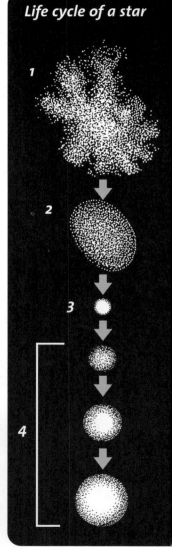

Life cycle of a star

1

2

3

4

1 Birth
2 Gas clouds shrink
3 Blue star starts to shine
4 Star expands

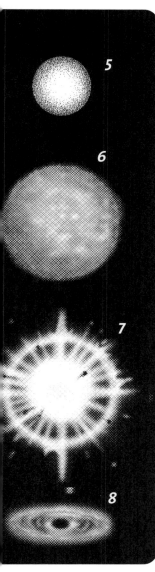

is the force of gravity in the case of celestial bodies. It may also be a mechanical force, such as that of a rotating lasso rope held by a cowboy.

The Sun has an average mass, which is described as "one solar mass." Other stars may contain as many as a hundred solar masses, or less than one solar mass. Stars similar to the Sun are described as dwarfs—the Sun being a yellow dwarf—while others are described as supergiants, giants, subgiants, and subdwarfs.

The mass and density of a star determine its size and brightness as well as how long it will "live." The nuclear reaction that produces a star's solar radiation is called fusion. This is the conversion of hydrogen to helium with the release of energy. Eventually, the star burns itself out.

STRANGE BUT TRUE

When stars burn themselves out they often become neutron stars, which are very dense balls of matter. The largest neutron stars have such a high density that their gravitational pull will not even permit light waves to escape. These are the black holes that form the hubs of every galaxy, constantly adding to their mass by feeding on other celestial bodies.

5 Red giant
6 Red supergiant
7 Supernova
8 Spinning pulsar

Death of a star

When stars run low on fuel they become unstable, resulting in their eventual collapse

Stars emit light in all directions.

As the star contracts, light near the surface is bent back into it.

When the star has a total grip on light emissions, only those at right angles escape.

As the star shrinks, all light is pulled back into it.

The final star has no light at all, and is known as a black hole.

© DIAGRAM

When clouds of matter known as nebulae condense in space, an interesting thing happens. Each particle is attracted to the others by gravitation, yet the atoms and molecules resist being crammed together.

THE RESISTANCE of atoms and molecules to coming together produces energy as an opposite force to gravitation, so a ball of matter becomes locked in a battle of forces. This battle is resolved by rotation. Gravitation translates into centripetal force, while the resistance translates into centrifugal force. In this way, spinning celestial bodies are conjured from a nebula. They include stars, planets, moons, and comets.

Stars are large gaseous spheres, made almost entirely of hydrogen and helium. It is the conversion of hydrogen into helium that produces the energy that stars emit as the form of stellar energy known as electromagnetic radiation.

Planets are often spheres of solid matter, although they can also possess shells and atmospheres comprising

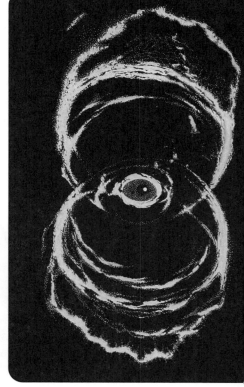

Hourglass nebula
This nebula has taken the form of two interlocking spheres.

The Near Earth Asteroid Tracking (NEAT) comet
Comets comprise balls of cosmic debris and ice hurtling through space.

liquids and gases. Planets orbit stars. Moons are similar, but they orbit planets and tend to lack liquids and gases as constituents of their composition.

Comets are largely made from ice and dust particles. When their orbits take them close to the Sun, their surfaces vaporize in the solar wind, so that they leave trails of debris in the opposite direction to the Sun. The solar system is also littered with asteroids, and chunks of mineral called meteoroids. When these enter the Earth's atmosphere they cause meteors, and fragments that survive to reach the Earth's surface are known as meteorites.

IT'S A FACT
It is commonly believed among scientists that planets and moons are made simultaneously with the birth of stars—the "nebular hypothesis." As the nebular mass begins to spin, the component materials become separated in order of density with the result that solids tend to aggregate into spheres orbiting the gaseous solar sphere. Over time, these orbiting spheres collide and rearrange themselves to become stable planets and moons. Asteroids and comets are fragments of matter generated by ancient collisions, that have found their own orbits.

Orion nebula
This nebula consists of an irregular cloud of matter.

© DIAGRAM

The Sun

The Sun is a yellow dwarf star, or G2 dwarf, to give it its technical name.

THE SUN IS 865,000 miles (1.4 million km) in diameter. At its core, the Sun's temperature is 27,000,000°F (15,000,000°C), but its surface is 9,900°F (5,500°C).

Its energy comes from a nuclear reaction called fusion; this occurs when hydrogen is converted into helium. The initial reaction is catalyzed by heat generated by gravitational pressure, but once started, the process is self-perpetuating. The Sun is considered to be about 4.7 billion years old, yet it still has plenty of fuel left. It comprises about 70 percent hydrogen by weight, 29 percent helium, and the remaining 1 percent is mainly made up from oxygen and carbon.

If the Sun were cut in two, it would be seen to comprise six distinct layers. At the center is the core, where the fusion process takes place. Around the core is a thick shell called the radiation zone. Next, there is a slightly thinner shell, named the convection zone. It is so called because convection currents keep this layer in constant turmoil.

Above the convection zone there are two thin atmospheric shells. The first is called the photosphere ("light ball") because

How the Sun formed
Gravitational pressure provided the energy to begin the process of fusion in the Sun.

Forming the Sun

Gravity pulled gases together to form the Sun

Intense heat inside the Sun created pressure which balanced the gravity

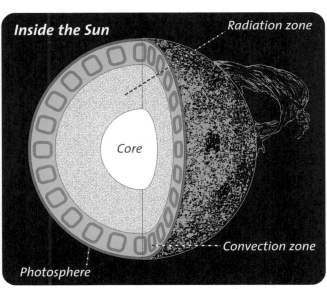

Inside the Sun

Radiation zone

Core

Photosphere

Convection zone

Inside the Sun (left)
The internal structure of the Sun is likely to be: photosphere, convection zone, radiation zone, and core.

it generates the Sun's light energy. The second is called the chromosphere ("color ball") because it gives the Sun its yellow color, where cooling takes place. Finally there is the corona. This may be thought of as the Sun's outer atmosphere, and is the emission of the Sun's energy in the form of electromagnetic radiation (light and "heat" waves), especially X-rays. The corona changes shape periodically. From the Earth, the Sun's corona is invisible to the naked eye, except on the occasions when there is a total solar eclipse.

IT'S A FACT
The electromagnetic radiation of the Sun has a wide spectrum, ranging from X-rays to gamma rays. In between there are visible light waves and invisible light waves— ultraviolet and infrared. The atmosphere of the Earth protects the surface from the most harmful radiation waves.

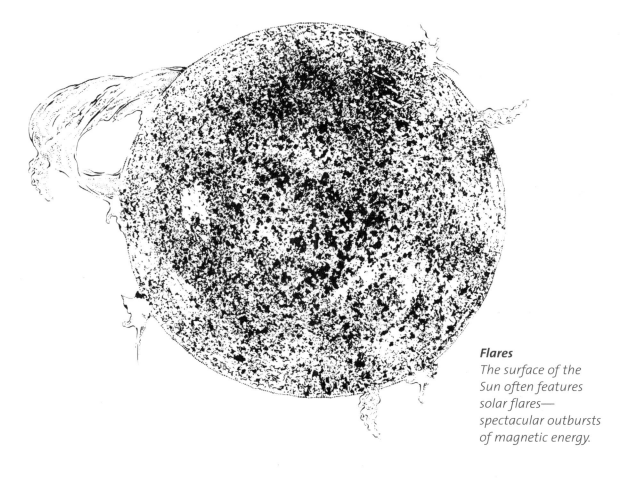

Flares
The surface of the Sun often features solar flares— spectacular outbursts of magnetic energy.

© DIAGRAM

In simple terms, the solar system is the Sun and all of its orbiting satellites. It is one of hundreds of billions of solar systems likely to exist in the universe.

THERE ARE NINE SATELLITES classified as planets. In order of distance from the Sun they are: Mercury, Venus, Earth, Mars, Jupiter, Saturn, Uranus, Neptune, and Pluto.

From the Earth, five of the other planets—Mercury, Venus, Mars, Jupiter, and Saturn—are visible to the naked eye, given the right conditions. For this reason, they have been known to people since antiquity. The other three planets are farther away, and were discovered only with the invention and development of the reflecting telescope. Uranus was first seen in 1781 by British astronomer William Herschel. Neptune was added to the list of planets

William Herschel

William Herschel
Herschel was one of the first scientists to realize the true immensity of the universe.

The planets in our solar system

Mercury

Venus

Earth

Mars

Jupiter

Saturn

Uranus

Neptune

Pluto

in 1846 by German astronomer Johann Galle, although Frenchman Joseph de Lalande had first reported a sighting in 1800. Finally, Pluto was found in 1930 by U.S. astronomer Clyde Tombaugh, having had its existence calculated by fellow American, George Forbes in 1880. Forbes had dubbed it "Planet X," and lived to witness its discovery fifty years later.

DID YOU KNOW?

Although all of the planets, except Mercury and Venus, have moons, there are many other celestial bodies in the solar system. Between the orbits of Mars and Jupiter there are many thousands of rocky satellites known as asteroids or minor planets and planetoids, depending on their size. They orbit the Sun as the "asteroid belt." Some asteroids have eccentric (elliptical and off-center) orbits, but the most eccentric orbits belong to comets.

© DIAGRAM

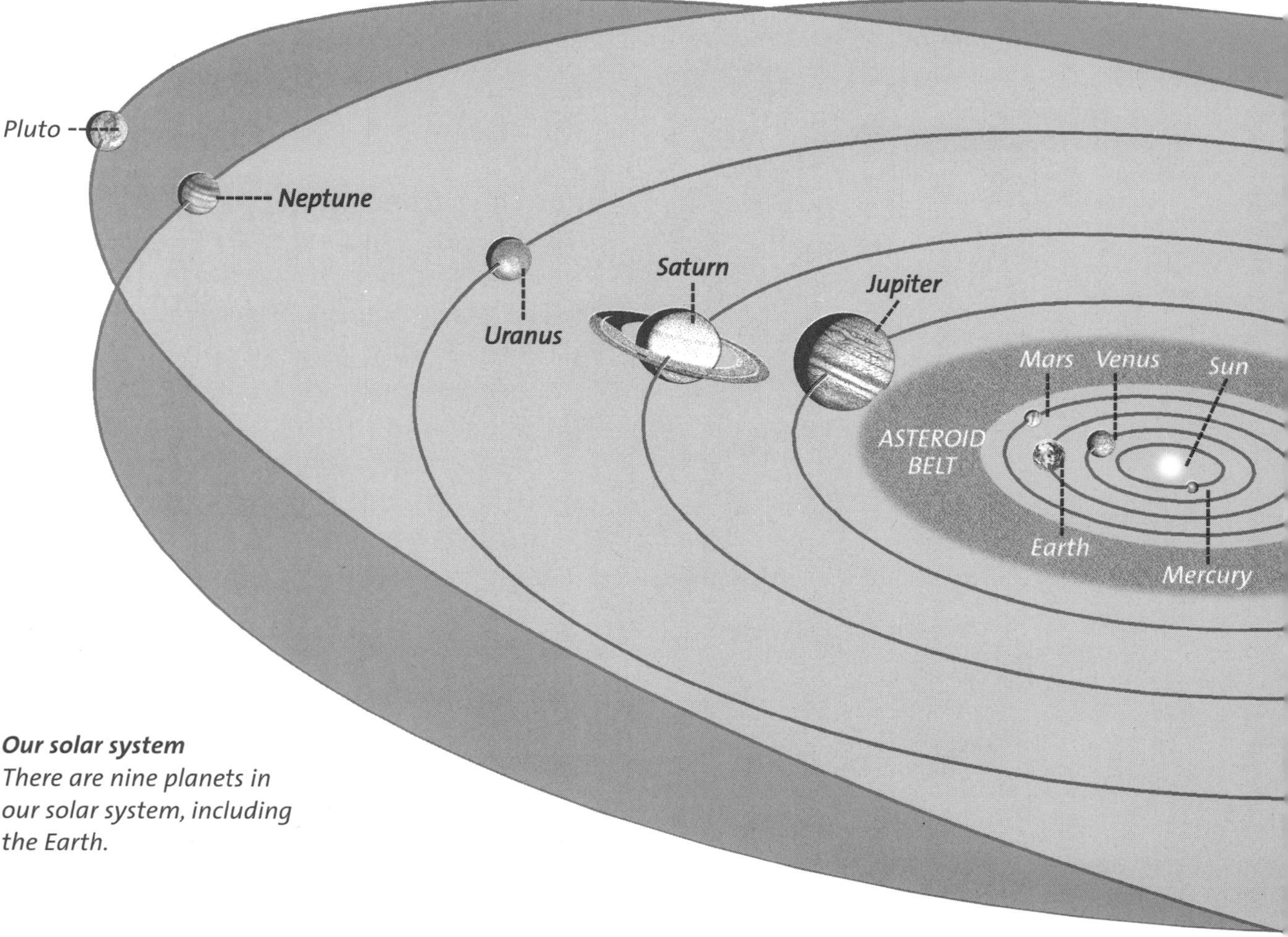

Pluto

Neptune

Uranus

Saturn

Jupiter

Mars Venus

Sun

ASTEROID BELT

Earth

Mercury

Our solar system
There are nine planets in our solar system, including the Earth.

Nine satellites, classified as planets, orbit the Sun, and are usually listed in relation to their distance from it.

Mercury **The first planet**

This planet is named after the Roman god Mercury, the messenger of the gods. It is only occasionally glimpsed in the night sky. Mercury has a crust comprising silicate rocks, but its core is made of iron. There is also a slight atmosphere of argon and helium.

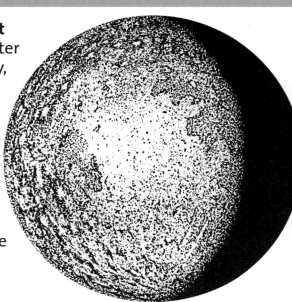

Venus **The second planet**

This planet is named after Venus, the goddess of love in Roman mythology. The planet glows brightly on a clear night or day. Its atmosphere is largely carbon dioxide, which is very dense and traps solar radiation. It has an atmospheric pressure 90 times that of the Earth, and its surface temperature can reach as high as 896°F (480°C).

IT'S A FACT

The surface area of the smallest planet in our solar system, Mercury, is approximately equal to the combined land areas of Asia and Africa.

Mars The fourth planet

This planet is named after Mars, the Roman god of war. This is because of its reddish, fiery glow, which is due to minerals rich in iron oxides in its crust. It has long been regarded as the planet most likely to harbor other life-forms because it possesses water, albeit frozen into ice caps. It also has an atmosphere containing both carbon dioxide and oxygen, even though it is so thin that its atmospheric pressure is lower than 1 percent of that of Earth. It is very likely that astronauts, or cosmonauts, will set foot on Mars before the close of the 21st century.

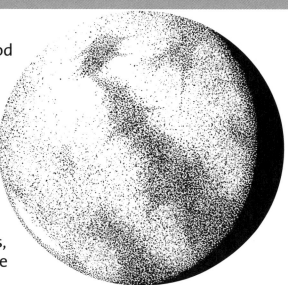

Jupiter The fifth planet

This planet is named after Jupiter, the supreme Roman god of gods, because of its giant size and its entourage of many moons. It can be so clearly seen at times that Chinese astronomers observed its larger moons with the naked eye in the 4th century C.E. Its turbulent atmosphere comprises a mixture of hydrogen and helium gases above an ocean of liquid hydrogen.

IT'S A FACT

At a steady jogger's pace of 6 miles per hour (9 kmph), it would take 173 days to go around the equatorial circumference of the Earth, and more than 5 years to go around the circumference of the largest planet, Jupiter.

© DIAGRAM

Saturn is visible to the naked human eye from the Earth. However Uranus, Neptune, and Pluto are visible only with the aid of a telescope.

Saturn **The sixth planet**

This planet is named after Saturn, the Roman god of agriculture, because he was the father of Jupiter. Saturn has the distinction of being the only planet with a density lower than water, being made almost entirely of hydrogen. In 1610, the Italian scientist Galileo Galilei became the first person to observe Saturn through a telescope, and to discover its ring system.

Uranus **The seventh planet**

This planet is named after Uranus, the Greek god who was the first ruler of the universe. This name was appropriate when Uranus was discovered in 1781 as it was then believed to be the outermost planet of the solar system. In fact, it had been mistaken for a star for many years before William Herschel viewed it through a telescope and saw that it was a sphere reflecting light from the Sun.

IT'S A FACT
The Earth takes 365 days to go around the Sun once; this is called its sidereal period. The most distant planet, Pluto, takes 247 years.

IT'S A FACT
Not all planets rotate at the same speed. The Earth takes 23 hours 56 minutes to rotate, whereas Pluto takes 6 days 9 hours.

Neptune The eighth planet

This planet is named after Neptune, Roman god of the sea. This is because the planet has a blue-green hue, which is reminiscent of an ocean. Its existence was calculated before its discovery, because its gravitation was affecting the orbit of Uranus whenever their paths came into contact with one another.

Pluto The ninth planet

This planet is named after Pluto, the Roman god of the underworld, as it is so distant and dark. The planet is only two-thousandths the size of the Earth. In fact, it is so small that it is regarded a planet only because it has an independent orbit around the Sun. It is actually smaller than some of the other planets' moons, including that of the Earth.

© DIAGRAM

The Earth is the third planet from the Sun, and the fifth largest in the solar system.

The Earth (right)
Our planet is the only one so far known to provide a suitable home for life-forms.

The Sun's rays
When the rays of the Sun meet the atmosphere head on, they have less distance to travel to the surface.

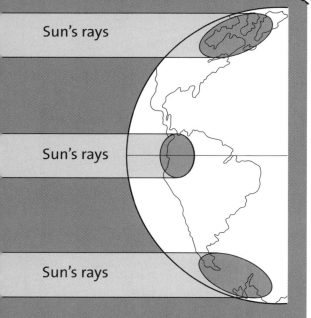

Sun's rays

Sun's rays

Sun's rays

THE EARTH ORBITS THE SUN at an average distance of 93.5 million miles (149.6 million km), has a diameter of 7,973 miles (12,756 km), and a circumference of 25,050 miles (40,080 km). The Earth takes 365.333 days to complete a single orbit of the Sun. This is a "solar year," but to equalize this with the calendar year, an extra day is added every four years—hence the 366 days of a leap year. The period we call a day is the time it takes for the Earth to complete a single rotation on its axis.

The Earth's axis is at an angle of 23.4 degrees from the orbital plane of the Earth, so that it tilts 46.8 (2 x 23.4) degrees in relation to the Sun during the course of the six months between mid-summer's day and mid-winter's day. It is the tilt that causes the seasonal changes, because it affects the depth of atmosphere that the Sun's rays need to penetrate to reach the Earth's surface. The tilt is also sufficient to prevent the Earth's poles from receiving any sunlight at all for three months of each year, alternately.

A defining characteristic of Earth is that it is home to life-forms. It may be unique in this respect. Of the many incidentals that allow for this phenomenon, distance from the Sun is important. The Earth's distance from the Sun happens to provide the Earth's surface with temperatures falling between parameters slightly above and below the melting point of water. These temperatures range from about -58°F (-50°C) to about 168.8°F (76°C), giving an average of about 55°F (13°C).

DID YOU KNOW?
Life-forms could not survive without water in its liquid form. Among other things, water acts as the medium for carrying and moving vital chemicals in the bodies of animals and plants. Around 70 percent of the Earth's surface is covered by water and, by volume, it accounts for a remarkable 95 percent of the living space for the planet's flora and fauna.

Yearly cycle
Over the course of six months the Earth leans toward, and then away from, the Sun by 23.4°.

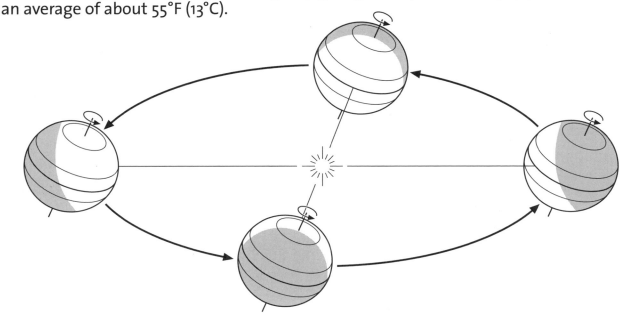

© DIAGRAM

The Moon is the Earth's only natural satellite.

THE MOON IS ONE FIFTIETH the size of the Earth by volume, and orbits at a distance of 238,857 miles (384,403 km). It orbits the Earth over a period of roughly 29.53 days—a lunar or synodic month, or lunation—and it rotates about its axis over exactly the same period. The result is that the Moon appears from the Earth not to rotate at all, so that we always see the same hemisphere. The other hemisphere is often termed the "dark side" of the Moon because we never see it, but it does actually receive as much sunlight as the "light side."

Although the Moon is the brightest object in the sky, next to the Sun, it does not emit light. Instead it reflects light from the Sun, just like the other planets and their own moons. The amount of the Moon visible depends on the angle it is observed at in relation to the Sun, and whether or not it is night or day. This angle varies over the course of a lunar month so that we see a sequence of changes daily.

The Moon changes from a New Moon (totally dark) to a Full Moon (totally illuminated), and then back to a New Moon again to complete a cycle of phases. It is possible to see the regions of the Moon that are in shadow at certain times because the Earth itself reflects the light of the Sun. This is known as "earthshine."

A clear view
The Moon has almost no atmosphere, so it is possible to view its surface with clarity from the Earth.

Sea of Cold

Sea of Showers

Sea of Serenity

Oceans of storms

Kepler

Copernicus

Sea of Vapors

Sea of Crises

Sea of Tranquility

Sea of Fertility

Sea of Clouds

Sea of Nector

Sea of Moisture

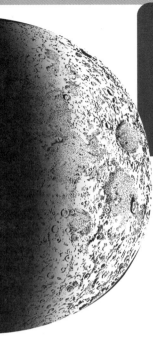

ECLIPSES

These can occur when the rays of light from the Sun are prevented from reaching one body by another.

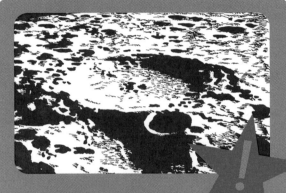

Lunar eclipse — Earth — Moon
Sun — Light

Solar eclipse — Moon — Earth
Sun — Light

Light and shade (left)
The spherical form of the Moon is evident whenever it is lit from the side.

A lunar month (below)
The Moon orbits the Earth completely every 29.53 days.

Phases of the Moon

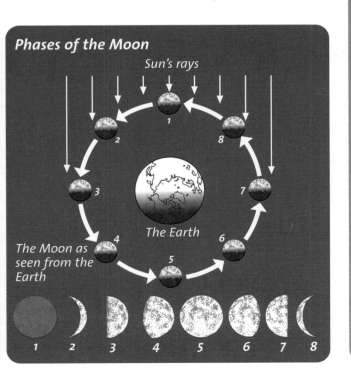

Sun's rays

The Earth

The Moon as seen from the Earth

1 2 3 4 5 6 7 8

IT'S A FACT

The Moon is a solid body, made from igneous rocks, which include compounds, such as silica, and oxides of iron, aluminum, calcium, titanium, and magnesium. Its atmosphere is so thin it is almost nonexistent, and not enough to subject its surface to dynamic processes. It maintains a clear record of its many meteor strikes in the form of craters littering its surface, unchanged for millions of years. Surface temperatures vary between -274°F (-170°C) and 230°F (110°C). Ice has been discovered at the Moon's polar regions.

Earth is thought to comprise different layers. At its very center there is a core sphere, made from solid iron and nickel.

THE SOLID CORE OF THE EARTH is calculated to have a radius of about 870 miles (1,400 km). It is responsible for the Earth's magnetic field and is thought to have rotated within the Earth on several occasions because the magnetism of some rock layers is the reverse of other layers. The core sphere is surrounded by a core shell, or outer core, made from molten iron and nickel, about 1,243 miles (2,000 km) thick. Enveloping the core shell are two mantle layers, comprising together about 1,864 miles (3,000 km) of rock, the lower layer solid, and the upper layer semi-solid. Finally there is the Earth's crust, which is made from solid rock. The crust varies in thickness, but is an average of 4 miles (6.4 km) thick at the ocean floor, and 25 miles (40 km) on land.

Inside the Earth
This diagram illustrates how the Earth would look if it were cut open into two equal halves.

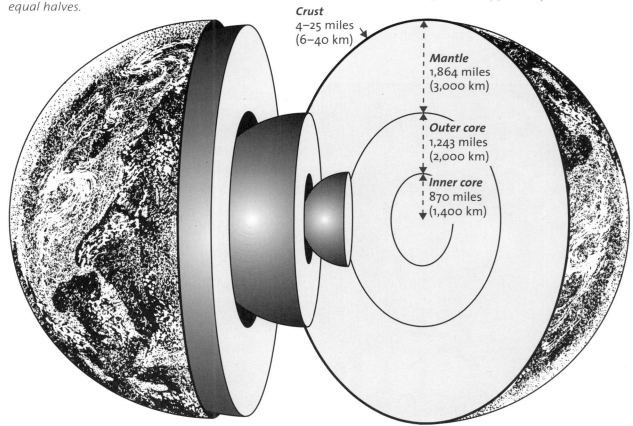

Crust
4–25 miles
(6–40 km)

Mantle
1,864 miles
(3,000 km)

Outer core
1,243 miles
(2,000 km)

Inner core
870 miles
(1,400 km)

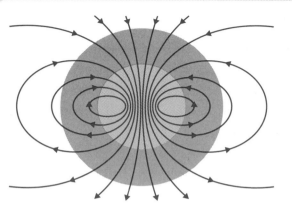

Magnetic field
*The heavy, iron core
of the Earth creates a
magnetic field.*

Between the crust and the upper mantle there is a region of molten rock, or magma, called the Mohorovicic discontinuity. It is the fluid boundary that allows for the phenomenon of tectonic drift, which causes the continents to be perpetually moving in slow motion. Magma is about 2,000°F (1,100°C). When it erupts at the surface it becomes lava, which flows until it cools sufficiently to begin solidifying. When this process is repeated over and over again, volcanoes are built up from the layers of lava. The Gutenberg discontinuity, positioned between the lower mantle and the core shell, allows for movement of the core.

The Earth's crust
*The outer layer, or crust, of the Earth is a shell
of solid rock which lies on a bed of molten
magma.*

Continental crust

Lithosphere

Oceanic crust

Magma

© DIAGRAM

The most basic components of the universe are atoms, which comprise sub-atomic particles called electrons, protons, and neutrons.

I T IS THE ARRANGEMENT of subatomic particles that determines the nature of atoms and, consequently, the elements they make. There are 112 elements so far discovered, 18 of which do not occur in nature. Although many elements occur in their pure, or native, form in nature, many more are too reactive and combine with other elements to form compounds. Compounds may comprise two, three, four, or more elements, so the number of possible combinations is enormous.

Matter, or the "stuff of the universe," is made from this vast number of elements and compounds. In theoretical physics, antimatter is a mirror image of matter, so that everything has an equal and opposite electrical charge, and so on. However, antimatter is not a part of our own world.

Elements and compounds generally exist in three different states: as solids, liquids, or gases. The world around us is made up from these three types of matter, because different elements and compounds vary in their melting and boiling points. A good example is water, particularly because it was used to

Electrons

Protons

Neutrons

Atom (above)
Protons, neutrons, and electrons comprise the subatomic particles of an atom.

Planet Earth (right)
We are surrounded by numerous different materials in solid, liquid, and gas form.

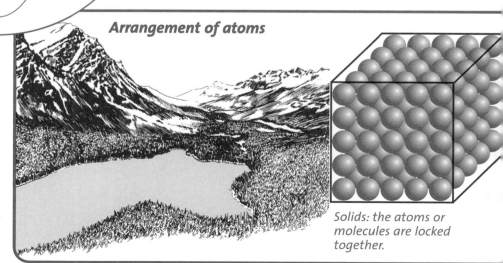

Arrangement of atoms

Solids: the atoms or molecules are locked together.

IT'S A FACT

Other materials behave in similar ways to water, but at different temperatures, so that the Earth is able to provide its familiar natural environment. Elements and compounds also undergo chemical reactions as conditions change, so that the composition of the lands, oceans, and atmosphere has been in a constant flux since the Earth's formation. This flux eventually led to the genesis of the first organic compounds—the raw materials of life.

calibrate the Celsius temperature scale, invented in 1742 by Swedish scientist, Anders Celsius (1701–44). Celsius divided the temperature range between the freezing and boiling points of water into 100 units. He called each unit a centigrade (Latin: hundredth-step). Thus the freezing and boiling points of water became 0°C (32°F) and 100°C (212°F) respectively. Below 0°C water is a solid (ice); between the two it is a liquid (water); and above 100°C it is a gas (water vapor).

Changes
Water adopts different forms at different temperatures.

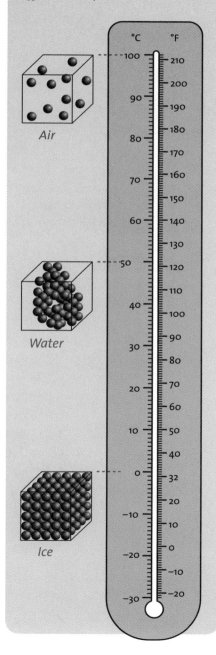

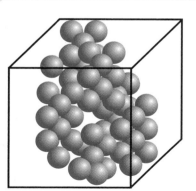

Liquids: the atoms or molecules can move over one another.

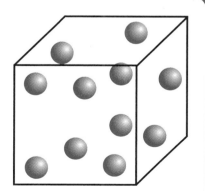

Gases: the atoms or molecules are independent of one another.

© DIAGRAM

Dynamic systems are the processes that keep the Earth's environment constantly changing. They are cyclical processes, which means that they repeat themselves perpetually.

THE TERM DYNAMIC SYSTEMS includes processes on a global scale, such as the hydrological (water) system, and the tectonic (continental drift) system. Others occur on smaller scales, such as the river, wind, glacial, groundwater, and shoreline systems. In combination they have kept the region of the Earth which we call the atmosphere constantly evolving since its formation about 4.3 billion years ago. From a human point of view, dynamic systems are not always immediately apparent, either because they operate at a very slow rate of change, or because they operate on a large scale which can be very difficult to visualize.

Before the modern age of science, people thought that the world was constant. They believed that the world had been created by divine means and had remained virtually unchanged since that time. However, scientists began to realize that this view was incorrect as exploration and discovery revealed more and more about the world around them. The most obvious clue that the world had changed over time was the abundance of fossil plants and animals to be found in rocks. In addition, fossils could be found in the most unlikely places, suggesting that the lands and oceans had moved about. Furthermore, the fossils showed that the Earth had witnessed different phases of climate, such as series of ice ages. The discovery of frozen mammoths in Siberia demonstrated that the last phase of ice age cold had occurred only a few thousand years ago.

Continental drift
The shapes of landmasses, their rock structures, and their fossils all demonstrate that the continents have drifted away from each other over a period of time.

5000 BCE   **Present day**

Saharan climate
A combination of land use by humans, and changing climate, has caused the Sahara to increase in size over a period of thousands of years.

IT'S A FACT

In 1972 the British scientist James Lovelock announced his Gaia hypothesis, named after *Gaia* (or *Gaea*), the mythological Greek goddess of the Earth. The hypothesis centered on the idea that the living environment of the Earth—the biosphere—functions in a similar way to an organism. That is to say, it defines and regulates the conditions necessary for the continued existence of life within it. Although this seems obvious, it introduced the notion of human responsibility for the management of the biosphere, such as the need to prevent global warming.

Texas fish
Fossils of aquatic creatures, such as this fish, show that certain places were once part of the ocean floor, millions of years ago.

© DIAGRAM

The first scientific attempt at explaining the movements of the continents came from American geologist Frank Bursley Taylor, in 1908. He proposed that two original landmasses—north and south—had collided with one another to form the continents, but the scientific community was reluctant to accept an idea with no scientific corroboration.

I N 1912 THE GERMAN ASTRONOMER, Alfred Wegener, put forward the first theory based on the idea of one original landmass, or supercontinent. He had support for his idea from British geologist Arthur Holmes in 1929, and South African geologist Alexander du Toit in 1937, but scientific proof failed to surface until the 1950s. A technique for measuring the magnetic orientation of rocks finally showed that Wegener had been correct in his assertion.

In addition to this magnetic proof, rock types and fossil types demonstrated that the continents had once been joined. When the continents are fitted together as a model it is immediately clear that they used to be conjoined because of the patterns in their geology (rock types) and the local distributions of fossil plants and animals. Additionally, the phases of fossils demonstrate just how the landmasses must have separated and rejoined at certain times in the past. Quite apart from anything else, the very shapes of the landmasses fit together

Ancient Earth
All of the land on the Earth used to be part of a single supercontinent which was surrounded by a single super-ocean.

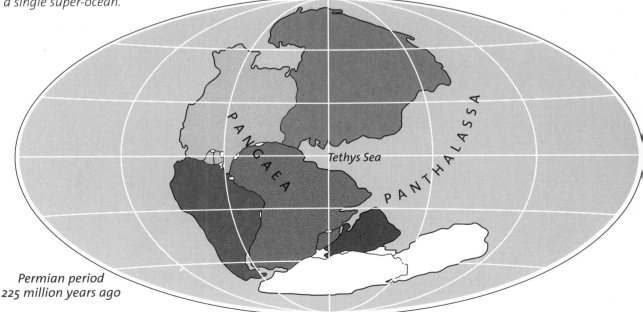

Tethys Sea

Permian period 225 million years ago

Triassic period
210 million years ago

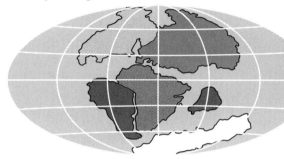

Jurassic period
150 million years ago

IT'S A FACT
Since then the continents have continued moving about and have rejoined in different places and at different angles, like leaves floating on water. In some places the continents have rucked up to form mountain chains.

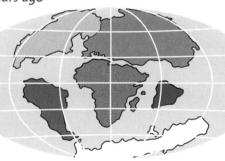

Cretaceous period
65 million years ago

with a reasonable degree of accuracy, allowing for coastal erosion, just like worn pieces of a jigsaw puzzle.

Wegener called the supercontinent Pangaea (Greek for "all land") and the ocean surrounding it Panthalassa ("all sea"). The current theory—continental drift—is that Pangaea divided into two pieces about 200 million years ago: Laurasia to the north, and Gondwana to the south. Eventually Laurasia subdivided into North America and Eurasia.

Similarly, Gondwana broke up to form South America, Africa, Australia, India, and Antarctica.

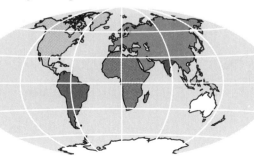

Present day

Continental drift is the phenomenon that explained to scientists why the continents seem to fit together like a giant jigsaw puzzle, even though they are spread over the globe. The processes by which continental drift occurs are known as plate tectonics.

THE PRINCIPAL TECTONIC PROCESS is convection in the magma layer (asthenosphere) beneath the Earth's crust (lithosphere). The crust is mainly a layer of cooled magma (igneous rock), naturally divided into roughly polygonal plates over the surface of the planet rather like a giant soccer ball stitched together from panels of leather. At certain points, convective up-currents force new magma to the surface. This forces the crust apart and pushes it away to make room. At other points, convective down-currents consume the crust. Thus, any landmass attached to a plate is gradually moved by the process.

When Alfred Wegener first proposed his hypothesis for continental drift in 1912, not even *he* understood the means by which it was actually happening. But advances in technology and scientific understanding had revealed the workings of tectonics by the 1960s. For one thing, it became possible to measure the distance between exact points to within a fraction of an inch (cm). This enabled scientists to demonstrate continental

➤	Plate movement
▲▲▲	Subduction zones
--------	Spreading ridges
———	Collision zones

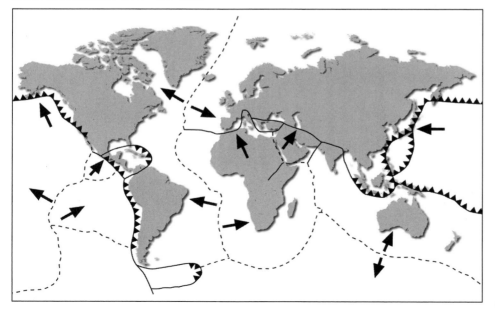

On the move (left)
Convection forces below the surface ensure that tectonic plates keep moving and changing shape.

Rift valley (right)
The Great African Rift Valley demonstrates what happens when the crust of the Earth is forced apart.

drift in action, by showing that some landmasses are drifting apart by several inches (cm) every year, while others are drifting together by similar increments. Also, better understanding of seismic activity—in the form of rift valleys, faults, earthquakes, and volcanoes—revealed that they were products of tectonic movements, so that a scientific model of continental drift could be described.

IT'S A FACT
The places where new crust is produced are called "spreading ridges" when they are located on an ocean floor. They are known as "rift valleys" when located on land. Examples are the Mid-Atlantic Ocean Ridge, separating the Americas from Europe and Africa, and the Great African Rift Valley, running down the eastern side of the African continent. The places where crust is being consumed are called "subduction zones." Examples can be found all around the Pacific Rim, and running through the Middle East, Asia, and Southeast Asia.

The rifting process (below)
There are three distinct stages in the process.

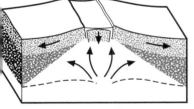

As the land is forced apart the central section slumps.

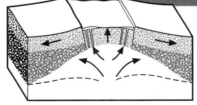

The central slump widens at its side.

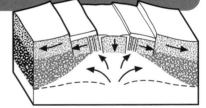

New slumps appear on either side of the original.

© DIAGRAM

Although the Earth's surface is scattered with landmasses, we know that there used to be just one giant landmass or supercontinent— Pangaea. This was surrounded by a universal ocean— Panthalassa.

PANGAEA WAS EVENTUALLY SPLIT by the Tethys Sea on its eastern flank, and divided into Laurasia and Gondwana. The continents subsequently fragmented and drifted over the globe. Some of them fragmented still further to create various island groups. The total land area accounts for about 30 percent of the globe's surface. This has reduced to a certain extent since Pangaean times, from perhaps 40 percent, due to coastal erosion and compression as the result of continental drift collisions. There are many islands, however, that have been created by volcanic activity. The largest volcanic island is Iceland, situated in the North Atlantic Ocean, but the vast majority are scattered through the Indian and Pacific Oceans. Although new crust is being generated all the time, it happens almost exclusively beneath

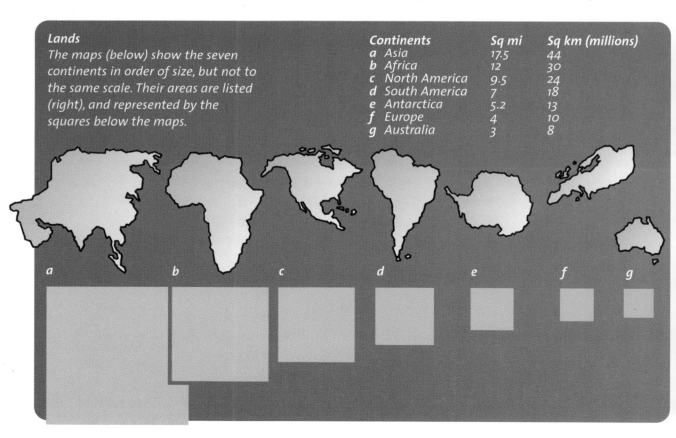

Lands

The maps (below) show the seven continents in order of size, but not to the same scale. Their areas are listed (right), and represented by the squares below the maps.

Continents	Sq mi	Sq km (millions)
a Asia	17.5	44
b Africa	12	30
c North America	9.5	24
d South America	7	18
e Antarctica	5.2	13
f Europe	4	10
g Australia	3	8

a   b   c   d   e   f   g

the four oceans of the world, so that new land is not created at any stage in the process.

There are seven major landmasses described as continents: Asia, Africa, North America, South America, Antarctica, Europe, and Australia. There are also thousands of islands. Some are large, such as Madagascar, Greenland, New Zealand, Borneo, Japan, Sumatra, Cuba, and Java. Others are small and often grouped together into archipelagos such as the Galapagos, Micronesia, the Philippines, and the Bahamas.

IT'S A FACT

There are four major oceans: the Pacific Ocean, Atlantic Ocean, Indian Ocean, and Arctic Ocean. The Southern, or Antarctic, Ocean actually comprises the southern regions of the Atlantic, Pacific, and Indian Oceans. Lesser bodies of water, partly or completely landlocked, are called seas or gulfs. These include the Mediterranean, the Caribbean, East China Sea, Sea of Japan, Gulf of Mexico, Gulf of California, North Sea, Red Sea, and Black Sea. The Caspian Sea is the largest landlocked body of water, with an area of 143,243 square miles (371,000 sq km).

49%

25%

22%

4%

Oceans	Area in square miles (sq km)
1 Pacific Ocean	63,800,000 (165,250,000)
2 Atlantic Ocean	31,830,000 (82,440,000)
3 Indian Ocean	28,355,000 (73,440,000)
4 Arctic Ocean	5,440,150 (14,090,000)

Oceans
The maps (above) show the location of the four oceans. Percentages indicate the proportion of the total world-ocean area made up by each named ocean. Their areas are listed (above right).

© DIAGRAM

Mountains are often the result of the Earth's crust crumpling, or rucking upward, where two tectonic plates are being forced together, such as has occurred in the Himalayas in Asia.

MOUNTAIN RANGES follow the line where two tectonic plates meet. Sometimes they include volcanoes. There are many mountain ranges over the world. As well as the Himalayas, there are the Andes in South America, the Rockies in North America, the Alps and Pyrenees in Europe, the Urals in Russia, and the Zagros in the Middle East, to name but a few.

Some formed when an oceanic plate collided with a continental plate. The outcome was a subduction zone marked by an oceanic trench where the oceanic plate slid beneath the less dense continental plate. Subducted lightweight rock that melted, punched up through the crust above to build volcanoes. Along with

A typical range (above)
An equal amount of rock usually lies unseen below the surface level of the mountains.

Rift zones (below)
The production of new crust forces the old crust together and creates mountains.

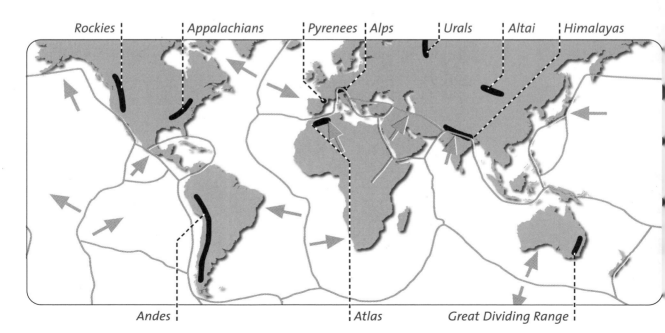

Rockies : Appalachians : Pyrenees : Alps : Urals : Altai : Himalayas

Andes : Atlas : Great Dividing Range :

sediments scraped off the oceanic plate, these formed the mountain ranges of western North and South America.

Mountain building takes millions of years because the tectonic plates are moving just a few inches each year. Having been formed, mountains are then subjected to the effects of erosion, so that they eventually assume their familiar rugged, jagged appearance. Evidence for the process of mountain formation can be seen in the mountains' sedimentary rocks. The layers of rock, or strata, originally laid down horizontally, are folded and distorted like layers of paper.

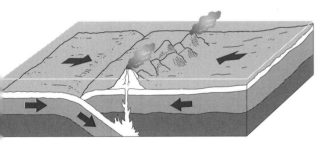

Volcanoes (above)
Subduction causes so much pressure that volcanoes vent magma from below.

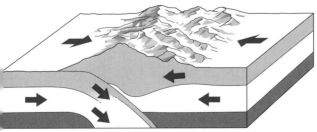

Mountains (above)
Some partly form from material scraped off subducted plates.

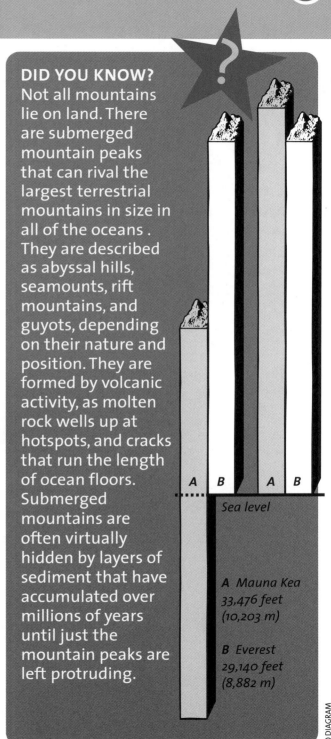

DID YOU KNOW?
Not all mountains lie on land. There are submerged mountain peaks that can rival the largest terrestrial mountains in size in all of the oceans . They are described as abyssal hills, seamounts, rift mountains, and guyots, depending on their nature and position. They are formed by volcanic activity, as molten rock wells up at hotspots, and cracks that run the length of ocean floors. Submerged mountains are often virtually hidden by layers of sediment that have accumulated over millions of years until just the mountain peaks are left protruding.

A B   A B

Sea level

A Mauna Kea
33,476 feet
(10,203 m)

B Everest
29,140 feet
(8,882 m)

© DIAGRAM

44 Rift valleys and spreading ridges

In places where the Earth is creating new crust, it does so by laying down roughly symmetrical strips of rock along fault lines. The process is called rifting. The results are rift valleys and spreading ridges.

MOST SPREADING RIDGES FORM beneath the oceans. Here the ridges flanking rifts originate as magma (molten rock) from beneath the crust. This magma solidifies into igneous rock called basalt when cooled by water.

Rifting occurs more commonly beneath oceans, simply because there the Earth's crust is far thinner, on average, than on land. As a result, the magma requires less upward force to break through. The consequence of rifting on land

Formed by tension

Formed by compression

Land slumping
In some places slumps occur because the land on either side has been pulled away; in other places the reverse is true.

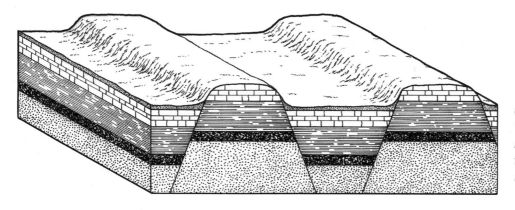

Undulations
When slumps occur in sequence, the terrain takes on an undulating surface.

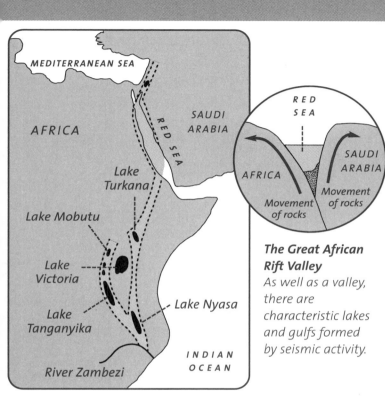

The Great African Rift Valley
As well as a valley, there are characteristic lakes and gulfs formed by seismic activity.

IT'S A FACT
A classic submarine rift valley is that which runs down the center of the Atlantic Ocean. For millions of years, it has been steadily separating the Americas from Eurasia and Africa by the continual production of new rock. It started life as a rift valley on land, which dissected the original landmass. Since then it has formed a vast oceanic basin, thousands of miles (km) wide, which is added to by just a few inches (cm) each year.

is that the land level falls below that of the surrounding terrain, so that the rift valley may acquire lakes. In landlocked areas the water will tend to be freshwater from the enveloping landscape so that lakes are formed. In places close to the edges of landmasses, the rift valley will ultimately breach into an ocean, so that a gulf is formed.

A good example of a landlocked rift valley is the Great African Rift Valley, which runs down the eastern side of the African continent. It includes several large freshwater lakes and volcanoes, including Mount Kilimanjaro. The volcanoes are symptomatic of seismic activity. The African Rift Valley is part of a system known as the Great Rift Valley, which continues northward into the Middle East. Between Africa and Arabia there is an example of a breached rift valley—the Red Sea—which connects to the Indian Ocean through the Gulf of Aden.

Typical volcanoes are mountains of cooled magma that has leaked from beneath the Earth's crust through fissures. The magma cools to form igneous rocks such as basalt and andesite.

WHEN MAGMA is partly, or newly, cooled it is known as lava. Lava can become frothed with volcanic gases while being ejected from a volcano, so that it cools as pumice, which will float on water. This occurs when the magma has a high silica content, because it is more viscous, and cools quickly before the gas bubbles have had a chance to escape into the atmosphere.

Classic volcanoes, which are known as "andesitic," are those with high silica levels. The lava tends not to flow very far before cooling so that the volcano takes the form of a steep-sided cone. With each new eruption the sides are coated with new lava and volcanic ash, so that the cone comprises alternate layers of lava and ash. When an eruption occurs it is because the pressure beneath the Earth's crust needs to be relieved. When the eruption happens there is usually little warning, because it is rather like a bottle blowing its cork.

Volcano Cerro de Lopizio, Mexico
This aerial image shows the mouth of the volcano, from which lava issues.

Volcanic activity
As well as the main volcano, the land is littered with minor volcanoes where the lava has seeped through ruptures in the shaken ground.

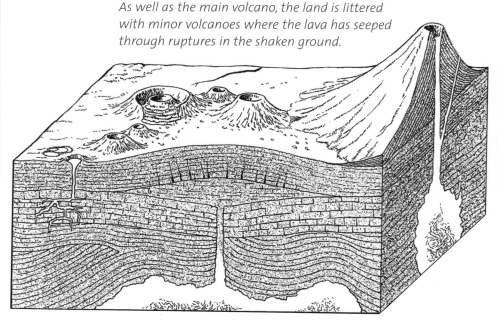

Following the initial explosion, a vast amount of material flows down the sides of the volcano. This is a mixture of superheated gases, volcanic ash, and fragments of lava, called a pyroclastic flow, which destroys anything organic in its path. Lava flows then race down the sides of the volcano, while ash and smoke ascend into the sky.

Volcanoes occur at places where seismic disturbance is a characteristic of the geology. Subduction zones and rift valleys are key locations, so volcanoes tend to form chains, following the line of tectonic activity. Those along subduction zones are typically andesitic volcanoes; those associated with rifting are known as shield volcanoes.

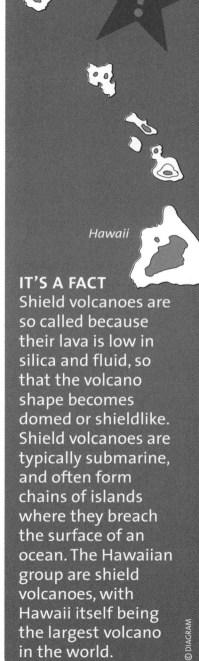

Hawaii

IT'S A FACT
Shield volcanoes are so called because their lava is low in silica and fluid, so that the volcano shape becomes domed or shieldlike. Shield volcanoes are typically submarine, and often form chains of islands where they breach the surface of an ocean. The Hawaiian group are shield volcanoes, with Hawaii itself being the largest volcano in the world.

© DIAGRAM

Lava sculptures
When lava reaches the surface it cools and solidifies, resulting in an array of different forms.

In the Earth's crust, seismic activity at subduction zones and rift valleys generally causes longitudinal movement—the landmasses are either heading straight toward, or away from, one another. However, fault zones tend to exhibit latitudinal movement, where one section of crust rubs sideways along the edge of another. It is at these places that the most severe earthquakes occur.

WHEN TECTONIC PLATES have been subjected to the processes of continental drift, they eventually reach a point where they need to adjust their positions to alleviate the mounting pressure. This is expressed in the form of compression and tension along fault lines. Unfortunately for people, these movements happen suddenly with no warning, because movement occurs only when sections of crust are ready to give. The movement is expressed as an earthquake, accompanied by a series of smaller aftershocks and tremors as the adjusted pieces of crust settle into their new positions.

We measure the severity of an earthquake on the Richter scale, named after the American geologist Charles Richter (1900–85). The scale is logarithmic, so that each full decimal level is thirty times the strength of the one below. A destructive earthquake

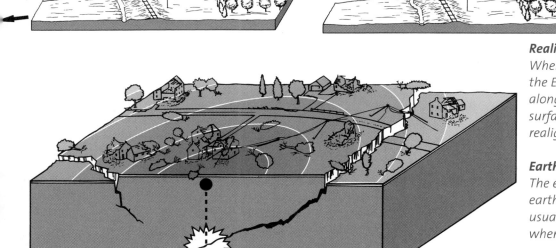

Realignment (above)
When two sections of the Earth's surface slide along a fault the surface may become realigned dramatically.

Earthquake (left)
The epicenter of an earthquake is not usually the place where most damage occurs to the crust.

can measure anywhere between 5.5 and 8.9 (the most powerful recorded in modern times) on the scale.

Earthquakes can affect a landscape profoundly. As well as the cracking of the surface to accommodate sideways movements, the fragmented surface can also be tossed about so that a formerly flat region may become terraced into plains at different levels and angles. In a wild setting this is assimilated into the scheme of things quickly enough by nature, but such changes can bring chaos to regions settled and farmed by people.

IT'S A FACT

When earthquakes occur beneath, or near, water the result is a shock wave called a tsunami (Japanese for "harbor wave"). Water cannot be compressed, so the energy of an earthquake is carried by the tsunami until it hits land and the energy is dissipated. Tsunamis have been responsible for annihilating many coastal settlements in the area around Japan, where submarine earthquakes are a common occurrence.

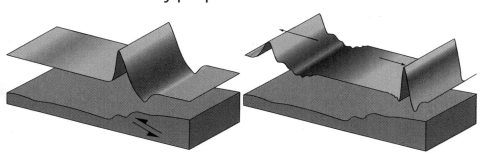

Tsunamis
Shock waves in the crust of the Earth give tsunamis their energy.

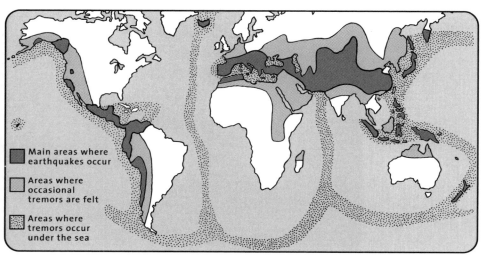

Main areas where earthquakes occur

Areas where occasional tremors are felt

Areas where tremors occur under the sea

Activity zones
This map shows the key areas of tremor and earthquake activity in the world.

© DIAGRAM

In the Pacific Ocean there are thousands of islands and seamounts created by submarine volcanoes, as the ocean floor is a "hotbed" of seismic activity.

VOLCANIC ISLANDS are those seamounts that have grown high enough to breach the water's surface. This is some achievement, bearing in mind that the depth of the Pacific Ocean can be several miles (km). Among them is the largest volcano on the planet—the island of Hawaii, in the north-central Pacific. Although oceanic spreading ridges generate new crust, new land is not often created, as the action typically occurs below sea level. Volcanic islands like Hawaii and offshore island arcs are valuable, therefore, because they are places where new land is created. However, some can also be destroyed by an explosive eruption, such as that on Krakatoa island in 1883.

Not all volcanic islands are simply volcanoes with their summits above water. Iceland is a volcanic island in the mid-North Atlantic that has been created by volcanic activity in the region of the Mid-Atlantic spreading ridge. In fact, Iceland is mainly built from magma spewed out from the ridge's

Pumice
Lava often solidifies with gas bubbles inside to form pumice, which floats in water.

Volcanic island
Iceland is the largest volcanic island which, even today, features volcanoes, hot springs, and geysers.

central fissure. The name "Iceland" alludes to the island's northerly latitude, resulting in its being largely covered by ice and snow. It might be better named "Lavaland" though, as it is almost entirely made from bare volcanic rock, and its volcanoes are still active.

IT'S A FACT

A curious phenomenon in the creation of volcanic islands is that a single volcanic fissure, or hotspot, can produce several islands to make a linear chain. This is because hotspots occur in the mantle beneath the crust or oceanic plate. Tectonic rifting causes the oceanic plate to move, while the hotspot remains stationary, so that volcanic activity at the hotspot results in a brand new volcano neighboring the volcano created the last time. The Hawaiian group is an example of this. Hawaii itself is the newest volcano, while the rest of the group trail off in a northwesterly direction. Each island in the chain is older the farther away from Hawaii it lies.

Creating volcanic islands

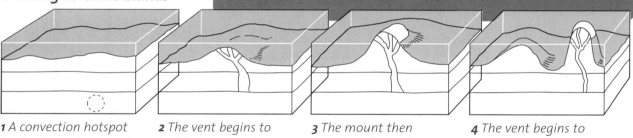

1 A convection hotspot begins to push upward.

2 The vent begins to build a seamount.

3 The mount then breaches the surface to form an island.

4 The vent begins to create a new island as the crust moves away.

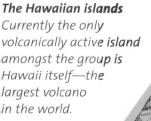

The Hawaiian islands
Currently the only volcanically active island amongst the group is Hawaii itself—the largest volcano in the world.

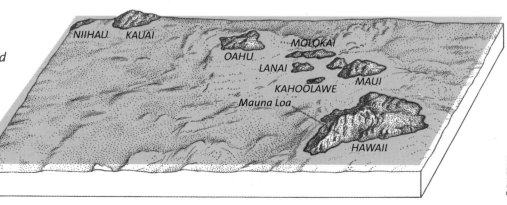

© DIAGRAM

Delta landscape
Rivers can create vast areas of new land called deltas.

WHEN THE WATERS OF A RIVER begin to slow, the result is that transported particles are left behind because the water lacks enough energy to carry them. This is called deposition. The slower the river, the smaller the particles it can transport, so that they are deposited in order of size, i.e., gravel, silt, mud.

In places where a large river traverses a flat area of land, the tendency is for the land to become seasonally flooded as the river swells following high rainfall upstream. The river has enough energy to transport greater quantities of material, which ends up deposited over the land. Over time, the area becomes coated with deposited material to become a level floodplain.

Floodplains are often near the places where rivers terminate in a sea or ocean, because rivers are at their largest and slowest when approaching sea level. Eventually the floodplain begins to extend itself beyond the existing land to fill the estuary.

The process of erosion, particularly by water, is responsible for breaking down mountain rock into smaller and smaller fragments. Eventually, the particles are small enough to be carried by streams and rivers to lower ground. This is called transportation.

Floodplain
As the river creates a floodplain it slows itself down and begins to meander over the surface.

When this happens it is called a delta. It is so called because "delta"—the fourth letter in the Greek alphabet—has a triangular appearance (Δ), which is roughly the same shape. Deltas are one of nature's ways of creating new land. In effect the river system has moved mountains into the sea, albeit over an extremely long period of time, and a little at a time.

Creating a delta

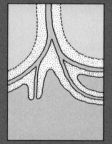

Stage 1
The river begins by sending out "fingers" of sediment.

Stage 2
Lagoons and salt marshes gradually appear.

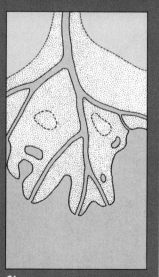

Stage 3
Eventually the delta is solid enough to qualify as "dry land."

DID YOU KNOW?
Deltas are not always triangular in shape because wave action and currents sculpt the deposits randomly. The Mississippi delta is described as a bird's-foot delta, because it has been divided and fragmented by distributaries and coastal erosion, giving it a rather asymmetrical and messy outline. The Nile delta, however, is a classic triangular shape, with almost perfect symmetry. This is due in part to the Mediterranean, which has only slight tides, and relatively calm waters.

© DIAGRAM

The term "fault" is used to describe any fracture plane between two sections of rock, along which each can move independently. However, faults vary greatly in scale, so they are divided into three groups: primary faults, secondary faults, and tertiary faults. They all arise from tectonic movements in the Earth's crust.

PRIMARY FAULTS are those found along divergent plate boundaries, where new crust is being produced by rifting. Primary faults run roughly perpendicularly, so that the boundary lines themselves are broken into many sections. This means that the tectonic plates can move apart a section at a time, rather than in one go. Primary faults typically lie beneath oceans, which their associated rift valleys have created. The California coast in North America is one of the few places where primary faults meet land. This is why the area is so prone to major earthquakes, which happen whenever movement occurs along one of the fault lines.

Secondary faults are found in places where plate boundaries are less well defined. They are rather like the cracks in a broken piece of glass. Southeast Europe and the Middle East have a system of secondary faults that are the result of a twisting movement between the Eurasian and African plates. These secondary faults

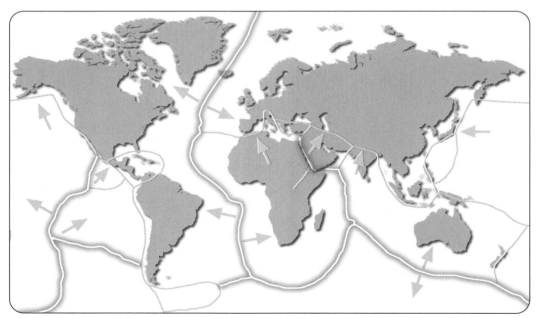

Fault lines
The surface of the Earth is littered with primary fault lines radiating from the tectonic plates.

Divergent plate boundaries

Faults

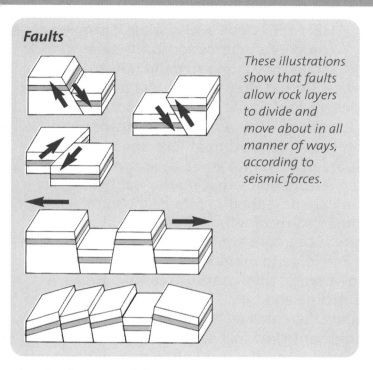

These illustrations show that faults allow rock layers to divide and move about in all manner of ways, according to seismic forces.

divide the crust like a jigsaw puzzle, and seismic activity is responsible for earthquakes and volcanoes in the region.

Tertiary faults occur on a far smaller scale than primary and secondary faults, but they are far more numerous. If it were possible to take a cross-section of any area of land, then tertiary faults would be evident in most places. They result from subtle movements of the layers of rock (strata) so that sections crack away and shift up or down in relation to each other. In places such as cliffs, quarries, and mine shafts it is possible to see examples of this because cross-sections are laid bare. The rock layers are often distinct, because they make patterns, so it is possible to see exactly how the sections of rock have used a tertiary fault to change their positions.

IT'S A FACT
Tertiary faults allow much of the energy generated by the Earth's seismic activity to dissipate without causing earthquakes or tremors. They also allow the processes of erosion to work more rapidly by breaking the surface rock into fragments.

© DIAGRAM

As the term suggests, folds are layers of rock that have been folded by compression. A single layer of rock is called a stratum, while several layers are called strata.

WHEN TECTONIC MOVEMENTS apply compression forces onto the sides of rock strata they begin to bend upward or downward so that they take up less horizontal space. When folds occur on a grand scale they result in the formation of undulating landscapes and, ultimately, in the creation of hills and mountains.

Folds are divided into three basic types, depending on their nature. Folds that mark a subtle drop in horizontal elevation are described as monocline folds. Folds that produce a convex form, or hill, are described as anticline folds. Folds that produce a concave form, or depression, are described as syncline folds. In many situations the folds are far more complex, however, so they comprise combinations. A combination of anticline and syncline folds is often described as an overfold, where it creates an "S" shape in the strata. In places where a single anticline fold stretches gently over a large area it is called a dome. If a syncline fold stretches gently over a large area it is called a basin. Some areas feature many domes and basins, so that the landscape is warped or buckled.

Rock has the capacity to bend and flow, given sufficient pressure and time. This is why rock strata are able to produce

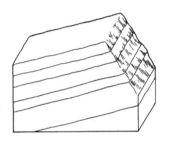

Rock strata
Layers of different rock are known as strata.

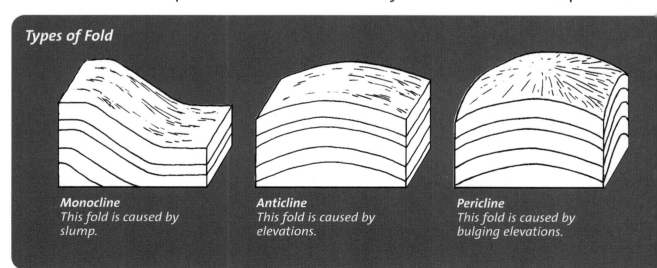

Types of Fold

Monocline
This fold is caused by slump.

Anticline
This fold is caused by elevations.

Pericline
This fold is caused by bulging elevations.

Sea cliff
Geologists can study rock layers more easily when they are exposed at cliff faces.

folds without cracking to pieces. Over geological time, rock behaves as a very viscous fluid, especially when it is rich in silica or quartz, which is a key component of igneous rocks. In some mountain ranges the folds can be extremely complex. This is because the pressures exerted on the rock strata were so great that they heated up, making them even more fluid. The result is that the folds resemble a piece of wrinkled cloth in cross-section.

DID YOU KNOW?
Cliffs and quarry walls are good places to observe folds in rock strata. In other places, such as mountainsides, they can be difficult to interpret as a result of the deposition of masking sediments.

Syncline
This fold is caused by bulging depressions.

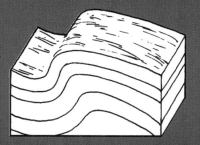

Overfold
This feature is caused by lateral compression.

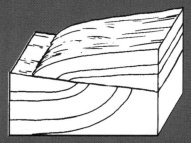

Nappe
This occurs when overfolds fracture along fault lines.

© DIAGRAM

Rock types

The crust of the Earth comprises many different types of rock. They differ as a result of the minerals in them, and also the ways in which they were formed.

THE MOST FUNDAMENTAL TYPES of rock are those formed by cooling magma as it rises to the surface of the Earth as lava in volcanoes or rift valleys. These are called igneous (fire) rocks. Their name is derived from the Latin word *ignis*, which means "fire," because they start life in an extremely hot, molten state. Most of the Earth's crust is made of igneous rock. A good deal of igneous rock is also formed by a process called plutonism, where magma cools into a solid while still beneath the crust. Both other types of rock are derived from igneous rocks, either directly or indirectly. The others are sedimentary (layered) rocks and metamorphic (altered) rocks.

The processes of erosion are responsible for breaking down igneous rock into progressively smaller fragments: boulders; rocks; stones; pebbles; gravel; silt; mud. Smaller fragments of rock are transported by water and deposited in layers elsewhere. Over time these layers get pressed together by the weight of material deposited above, until they once again turn

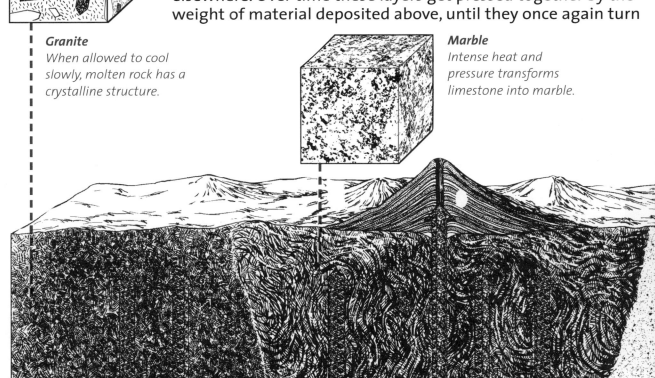

Granite
When allowed to cool slowly, molten rock has a crystalline structure.

Marble
Intense heat and pressure transforms limestone into marble.

into rock. These rocks are described as sedimentary rocks. This is because they originate from layers of sediment at the bottom of water bodies, such as lakes, seas, and oceans.

When sedimentary igneous rocks become subjected to greater pressures, from both weight above and seismic movements, they begin to heat up as their molecules get compressed. This causes chemical changes to occur so that the rocks transform into metamorphic rocks. They are so called because the rocks have metamorphosed from one type of rock into another.

Occasionally conditions result in conglomerate rocks—sedimentary or igneous or metamorphic rocks mixed with lumps of other rock. These rocks occur when the process of gradual deposition is interrupted, such as by a flash flood or volcanic eruption, so that the bottom of a lake or sea is scattered with debris.

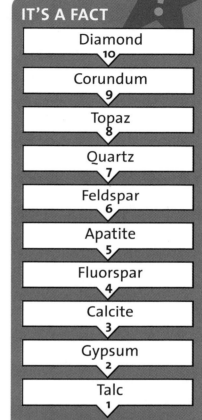

IT'S A FACT

| Diamond |
| 10 |
| Corundum |
| 9 |
| Topaz |
| 8 |
| Quartz |
| 7 |
| Feldspar |
| 6 |
| Apatite |
| 5 |
| Fluorspar |
| 4 |
| Calcite |
| 3 |
| Gypsum |
| 2 |
| Talc |
| 1 |

Mineral types can be sorted according to their hardness. This is done by using Mohs's scale, named after German mineralogist Friedrich Mohs. The scale runs from 1–10, with diamond as the hardest and talc the softest.

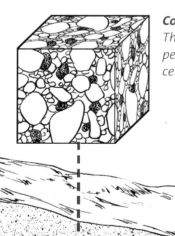

Conglomerate
This is an aggregation of pebbles and sand cemented together.

Igneous rocks are those rocks derived from magma, the molten layer beneath the Earth's crust.

Standing columns
Sometimes igneous rocks can cool slowly enough to form huge crystals, which then form standing columns when exposed by erosion.

THE WORD "IGNEOUS" is derived from "*ignis*," Latin for fire, as magma is hot and fiery when it spews from volcanoes as lava. Magma is a complex mixture of gases, solids, and liquids, and comprises a number of elements, such as aluminum, calcium, sodium, potassium, iron, and magnesium. However, the key constituents are silica or silicon dioxide (SiO_2) and water or hydrogen monoxide (H_2O). They control the properties of magma and therefore determine the character of the igneous rock produced as the magma cools. Silica accounts for 37–75 percent of magma's bulk. The higher the silica content, the higher the viscosity (resistance to flow) of the magma. The word "magma" is itself derived from the Greek word meaning to knead a mixture together.

When lava cools very quickly there is insufficient time for crystals to form. This results in rock with a very fine grain. Obsidian has such a fine grain that it has a glassy texture and appearance. Basalt and rhyolite have a slightly larger grain size, and are opaque in appearance. This is described as an aphanitic texture.

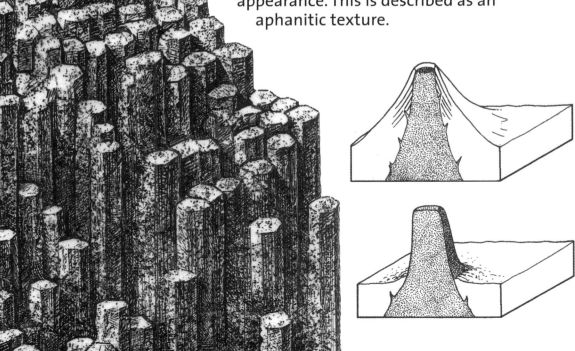

When lava is given longer to cool it forms crystals of quartz and feldspar. Some rhyolite contains these isolated crystals, called phenocrysts. This happens when periods of slow and rapid cooling alternate. They are said to have a porphyritic-aphanitic texture.

When lava cools slowly and at an even rate, crystals form in regular sizes. This is a phaneritic texture and is seen in typical granite. The crystals can vary in hue and tone, depending on the chemical impurities present, giving granite its range of colors. Some granite contains different-sized crystals, where cooling has been slow but varied in rate: it then has a porphyritic-phaneritic texture.

IT'S A FACT
Some igneous rock looks very similar to sedimentary rock. This is because it is formed from layers of volcanic ash and lava, compressed together. It is said to have a pyroclastic texture, after the pyroclastic flow down the sides of volcanoes from which it originates.

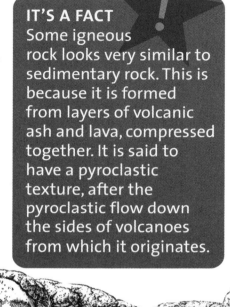

Man-made monuments (right)
In places where rock is thick, and also stable, it can be sculpted into enormous statues.

Volcanic plug (left)
If the core of an old volcano is more resistant to erosion than the shell (top), it will eventually become a volcanic plug as it is left exposed (bottom).

Sedimentary rocks originate from layers of sedimentary materials.

SEDIMENTATION TYPICALLY OCCURS at the bottom of still water bodies fed by rivers, such as lakes, seas, and oceans. It can also occur in slow-flowing rivers, estuaries, flood plains, and deltas. In addition, glaciers can deposit layers of debris, known as moraines. Also, fine-grained materials can be deposited by wind action in certain places. The materials deposited are usually particles of other eroded rock, although they can also be the inorganic remains of animal life. Sedimentary rocks typically have visible layers, or strata, in cross section, because the materials deposited vary over time.

Sandstone is a sedimentary rock made up from particles of sand, as the name suggests. The particles or grains can range in size, but are usually 0.004–0.079 inches (0.1–2.0 mm) in diameter. The sand particles may be quartz or feldspar from igneous rock, or from gneiss, a metamorphic rock. The grains form sandstone by adhering together using a natural cement

Chalk
This soft rock is made from the calcareous remains of planktonic animals.

Making coal
These illustrations show how a layer of organic sediment gradually becomes compressed by other layers until it eventually turns into coal.

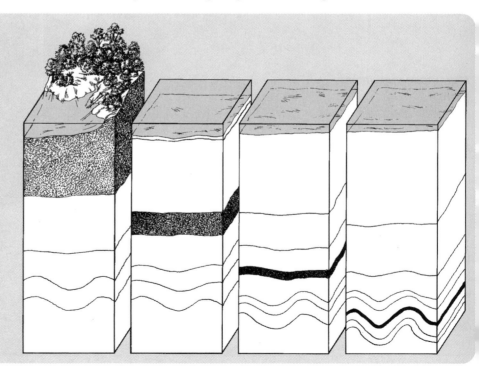

of silica, iron oxide, or calcite. Some sandstone contains the odd fragment of stone and is called lithic (stone) sandstone. When silt and mud turn to stone they become shale, siltstone, or mudstone. The particles of these stones are often too small to see with the naked eye.

Although sandstone, shale, siltstone, and mudstone can contain certain amounts of material from organic origin, limestone and chalk are almost entirely made of the skeletons and shells of ancient sea creatures. Chalks and limestones are principally made from calcium carbonate, but limestones contain the shells of larger creatures, making them denser and harder.

IT'S A FACT
In special conditions a rock called oolitic ("egg stone") limestone is created. It comprises grains of calcium carbonate coated with layers of yet more calcium carbonate, cemented together. This occurs when particles are moved about by wave action in water containing dissolved calcium carbonate, which is deposited by precipitation. The coated particles then accumulate to form the rock itself.

Limestone (middle)
This shelly rock contains larger animal remains than chalk.

Strata (left)
Different layers of sediment form distinct stripes called strata.

Grand Canyon (right)
The canyon is the result of water erosion through many layers of sedimentary rock.

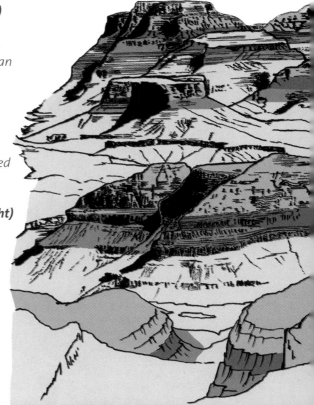

Metamorphic rocks have had their chemical and physical characteristics altered to become new types of rock. The process is called metamorphosis, or "change of form," and is principally the result of increased pressure and temperature, although the permeation of chemicals can also play a part.

WHEN LIMESTONES AND CHALKS are compressed, their constituent particles are forced together and become heated, with the result that they become denser and convert into types of marble. This is where the calcite has ultimately developed into hard crystals, so that the molecules are arranged in a tightly interlocked manner. Similarly, sandstone will become quartzite, where the quartz sand particles melt and recrystallize into a continuous mass.

Shale can undergo a series of alterations. Its initial change is into slate, which is harder than shale and divided into layers, or strata, by hairline cleavage planes. Slate will turn into schist, which is where the constituent minerals have begun to separate and crystallize. Finally, schist will turn into gneiss. This metamorphic rock looks similar to igneous rock because the constituent minerals

How metamorphic rocks are formed

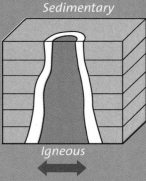

Sedimentary

Igneous

"Contact" rocks occur when igneous rocks intrude through sedimentary rocks; metamorphic rocks are formed at the point of contact.

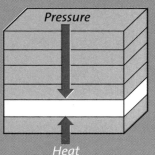

Pressure

Heat

"Regional" rocks are formed when layered rocks come into contact with high temperatures from below, and also high pressures from above.

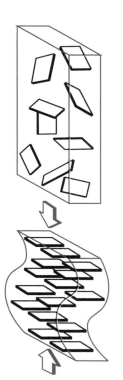

New rocks from old (right)
Heat and pressure can transform original rocks into fine-grained granular or foliated rocks.

Foliation (left)
In shale the tiny flakes of mica are not arranged in a regular position. After the process of foliation, (i.e., alignment by directed pressure) they align to form layers, as happens in slate.

have melted and fully crystallized in the same manner as slowly cooled magma. The original rock, from which a metamorphic rock has been derived, is called the parent rock—in this case the parent rock is shale.

Rhyolite, granite, and basalt are all igneous rocks that can be metamorphosed into forms of schist. Granite can also become changed into amphibolite, which comprises minerals called hornblende and plagioclase. Hornblende is a silicate-rich, translucent mineral, with ripples of color resembling polished horn or tortoiseshell. Plagioclase is a silicate containing aluminum, which is opaque and whitish. It is not unknown for conglomerate rocks to become metamorphic. Fittingly, they are then described as metaconglomerates.

IT'S A FACT
Rocks become metamorphic by degrees, depending on the pressures and temperatures to which they are exposed. It is possible, therefore, to discover something of the past tectonic activities in a region by looking at the ways in which the parent rocks have altered.

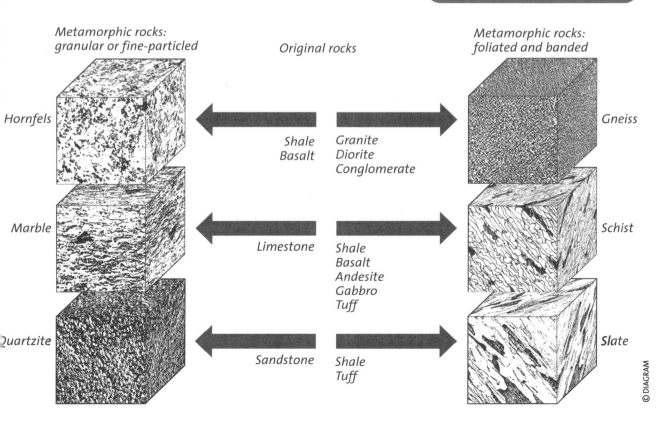

Metamorphic rocks: granular or fine-particled

Original rocks

Metamorphic rocks: foliated and banded

Hornfels — Shale / Basalt ⟷ Granite / Diorite / Conglomerate — Gneiss

Marble — Limestone ⟷ Shale / Basalt / Andesite / Gabbro / Tuff — Schist

Quartzite — Sandstone ⟷ Shale / Tuff — Slate

© DIAGRAM

Conglomerates and breccias

Conglomerates and breccias are sedimentary rocks containing collections of different rock fragments cemented together. They lack uniformity in grain size and are created in places where the processes of sedimentation are unregulated: the material is deposited in a turbulent manner, which is why the grains are irregular sizes.

CONGLOMERATES AND BRECCIAS are common on the floors of ancient cave systems. When caves breach the surface of the land under which they have been created, they form sinkholes when their ceilings collapse. At times of rainfall and flooding, water drains into the sinkholes, carrying all manner of debris with it into the cave. Here it accumulates—having nowhere else to go—and then gradually turns into conglomerate or breccia rock. A combination of weight from above and the permeation of naturally-cementing chemicals

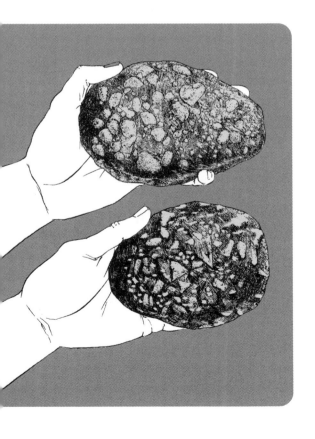

Forming caves (right)
Rainwater trickles down through crevices in limestone (top); it then dissolves the rocks it touches (middle); streams plunging underground widen crevices into caves (bottom).

Natural concretes (left)
Conglomerate has rounded clasts (top); while breccia has sharp-edged clasts (bottom).

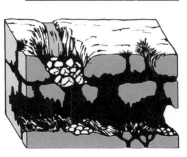

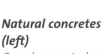

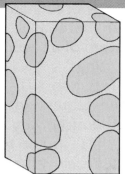

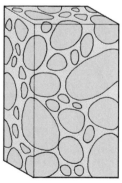

Composition (above)
Conglomerates vary in the proportion of fragments and cement that they consist of.

IT'S A FACT
Conglomerate rocks also form in the bases of mountains and hills following landslides, which churn up the substrate to form concretions. Also, the moraines left by retreating glaciers are similar mixes of rock, stones, gravel, and soils that have been removed from the landscape and dumped.

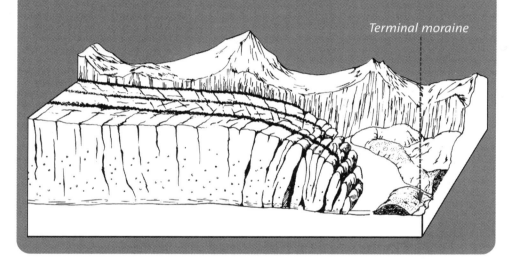

Terminal moraine

cause the particles to adhere together. The precipitation of calcium carbonate, between the particles or forming layers, is known as tufa. Conglomerates contain mixed-size round fragments of rock. Breccias contain medium-sized sharp-edged fragments.

Most conglomerate rocks are formed on the beds of streams. Over time, large fragments of rock settle on the bottom, and act as dams to catch other pieces of rock. Eventually the bed is formed from a collection of rock fragments of varying sizes, because the flowing water cannot transport them farther along. The water then provides cement, in the form of dissolved minerals, such as calcium carbonate and iron oxide, which glue all of the particles together into a concretion. "Concretion" comes from the Latin word *concrescere*, meaning "to grow together."

© DIAGRAM

Not all fossils originate from the remains of animals and plants. It is also possible for inorganic details to become preserved as fossils. This is known as feature fossilization. These kinds of fossil are not mineralized (petrified) objects, but castings of surface features present at the time when sediments were deposited over them.

FEATURE FOSSILIZATION occurs on different scales. When material is deposited at the bottom of a cave, lake, or sea, then the resulting sedimentary rock is, in effect, a fossil casting of the shape of the depression. Depression castings can therefore vary in size, from just a few inches (cm) up to several miles (km). Sediments can also record the surface details of a landscape. For example, the ripples on mud or sand are often seen in sedimentary rocks. Sometimes even the marks left by raindrops are preserved. Volcanic ash can be

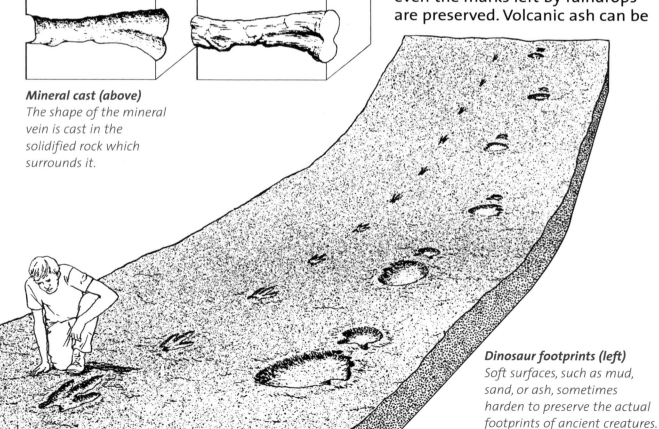

Mineral cast (above)
The shape of the mineral vein is cast in the solidified rock which surrounds it.

Dinosaur footprints (left)
Soft surfaces, such as mud, sand, or ash, sometimes harden to preserve the actual footprints of ancient creatures.

a good medium for recording such subtle details. This is because it is light and powdery when it first settles, but then sets firm once it has become wet. Subsequent layers of ash then blanket, and preserve, the surface.

In caves it is even possible for material to make casts of overhanging features. If a cave completely fills up with material then this is inevitable, but it can also be done in another way. When water seeps through from above it is often rich in dissolved calcium carbonate. The calcium carbonate precipitates from the water in very thin layers, as it runs over surfaces, to form a type of rock called tufa. Tufa is not dissimilar to plaster of Paris in the way it will coat things to form concave or convex molds of their shapes.

IT'S A FACT
Features can also become fossilized by igneous intrusion. This is when molten rock, or magma, is injected into fissures and voids from below. Having filled the available space, it solidifies by cooling down. Of course, lava from volcanoes will also envelope surface features before solidifying. Lava also has a habit of preserving details of its own history, such as the way it moves, and cools, once exposed at the Earth's surface.

Preserved in ash
When volcanic Mount Vesuvius erupted in Roman times, the ash fell so quickly that it formed casts of the deceased people and animals in the town.

Stone trees (left)
The stumps of fossilized trees are exposed as the rock surrounding them is eroded away.

© DIAGRAM

A fundamental geological process is that of rock erosion. Rocks are combinations of minerals that can ultimately be broken down, and separated, by different means of erosion.

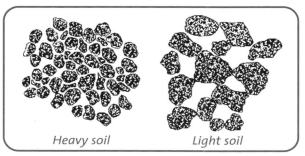

Soil density (above)
Heavy soil tends to consist of small particles with little air between them, while light soil consists of larger particles and more air spaces.

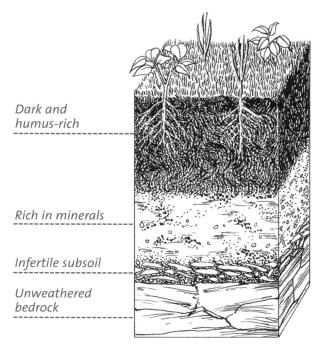

Dark and humus-rich

Rich in minerals

Infertile subsoil

Unweathered bedrock

ROCKS START TO BREAK DOWN in places where they are exposed to the elements—especially water—such as mountain tops, coastal cliffs, and cave systems. Bedrock is rock in its original state, as a continual mass, forming the basis of any landmass. The process of erosion can be simplified into a sequence, according to the size of the rock: bedrock; boulders; rocks; stones; pebbles; gravels; soils; silts; muds; solutes. Solutes are the constituents of rock that have actually dissolved in water, such as the salt in the water of the oceans.

The processes of erosion can be divided into two areas: physical erosion and chemical erosion. Physical erosion involves the breakdown of rock by wear and tear. On mountaintops ice is responsible for levering boulders away from the main mass of bedrock. Once freed, the boulders tumble down the mountainside to be smashed to smithereens at the bottom. The rock fragments then begin their journey farther downhill, pushed and carried by flowing water, all the time knocking into one another and breaking into smaller and smaller pieces.

Soil formation (left)
A cross-section of substrate shows that soil is layered from the bedrock to the surface.

IT'S A FACT

Living creatures are essential in the formation of soil. Their droppings and bodily remains help to form humus, the dark fertile matter in soil. Plant remains also contribute to this.

Creatures which help to form soil

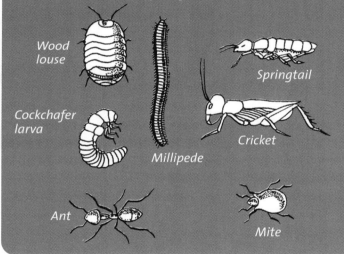

Wood louse

Springtail

Cockchafer larva

Cricket

Millipede

Ant

Mite

Eventually they break down into pieces that are so small that they are described as sand or mud, which form soil when mixed together. When rock fragments are so small they have a very high surface area to volume ratio, making it easier for water to dissolve and release minerals vital for life-forms, which is why soils are described as fertile. When rock dissolves in water it is known as chemical erosion. Some types of rock dissolve far more easily than others, especially when high in carbonates.

Soil types

Tundra soil

Desert soil

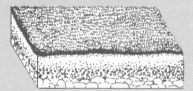

Chernozem soil

Ferralsol soil

Brown forest soil

A red-yellow podzol

© DIAGRAM

Yellowstone Park, Wyoming

Eroded landscapes (above and right)
The actions of water, wind, ice, and fluctuating temperatures all play their part in sculpting the landscape by the processes of erosion.

Bryce Canyon, Utah

Physical erosion is the wear and tear of the landscape by the elements or weather —rocks are worn down into their constituent parts. The principal agents responsible for physical erosion are water, temperature, and gravity.

ON MOUNTAIN PEAKS water finds its way into cracks between rock layers (strata). When this water freezes it turns into ice and expands. The expansion forces the rock apart until boulders break free and tumble down the mountainside, causing further disintegration of the rock as it strikes other rocks on the way down. Melt waters then create mountain streams, which begin transporting pieces of rock downstream. As the pieces of rock migrate along the streambed they become further abraded and fragmented, so that the water is able to carry the pieces still farther. In this way, mountains become worn down by physical erosion.

Glacier at Mt. Hayes, Alaska

Glaciation (above)
In consistently cold areas, ice rivers carve valleys into the landscape.

IT'S A FACT
Glaciers are also the cause of physical erosion. They are essentially rivers of ice which flow slowly but surely down mountainsides. As they move they carve out U-shaped valleys by physical erosion. Loose pieces of rock are frozen into the ice and then act like the teeth of a saw, scraping away at the bedrock. Fragments of rock also fall onto the ice and are carried along as if on a huge conveyor belt. The material is eventually dumped where the glacier terminates, so that flowing melt water continues the erosion process.

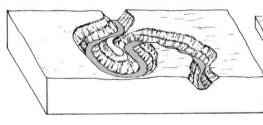
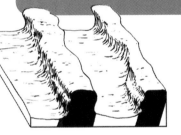

Wind can also be responsible for physical erosion. In desert areas winds blow soil away so that only sand is left behind. In turn the sand grains can eat away at the surfaces of rocks during sandstorms, so that the landscape becomes sandblasted. Waves on the surfaces of oceans are caused by the energy of wind transferred to the water. In coastal areas waves can batter the shore, causing extensive physical erosion during storms. In addition, wave action causes longshore-drift. This is where pebbles get transported along a coast. As they move along they rub against one another, gradually wearing away into smaller and smaller pieces of rock.

Wind and sand (above)
Given the right conditions, wind can blast rocks with sand particles, and erode the rocks away.

© DIAGRAM

Chemical erosion is the wear and tear of rock by chemicals alone, but it is always accompanied by physical erosion.

THE SIMPLEST FORM of chemical erosion is dissolution, where rock dissolves in water to become a solution, and is then carried away. The water is the "solvent" and the rock is the "solute." The best example is the salt carried by the world's oceans. Sodium chloride is a common mineral within many rock types. It dissolves into river water and is carried to the sea; it then becomes concentrated as the water continues its cycle of evaporation.

Other forms of chemical erosion also involve water, but in the form of acids. When carbon dioxide (CO_2) dissolves into water (H_2O) it becomes carbonic acid (H_2CO_3). Similarly, nitrous acid (HNO_2) is formed when nitrogen oxide gases—monoxide (NO) and dioxide (NO_2)—dissolve in water. Sulfurous acid (H_2SO_3) results from sulfur dioxide (SO_2) dissolving in water. Carbonic, nitrous, and sulfurous acids are all weak acids, by laboratory standards, but they are sufficiently strong to attack certain rocks far more rapidly than water alone. This form of erosion is known as hydrolysis. Acid rain comprises a mixture of these acids. The oxide gases dissolve in water droplets when rain clouds form from water

Tombstone (below)
Objects made from stone eventually show signs of erosion on their surfaces.

Limestone fragmentation

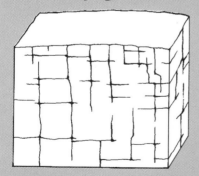

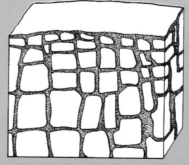

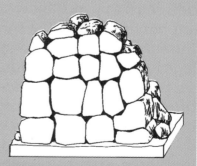

Stage 1
Surface water begins the process of erosion by seeping into cracks in the rock.

Stage 2
The cracks begin to widen into fissures as the water dissolves more rock.

Stage 3
The landscape eventually begins to collapse as boulders become separated by erosion.

vapor in the atmosphere. These oxides are present due to natural phenomena, but factories produce them in far greater amounts as the waste products of industrial processes.

Some types of rock change chemically when exposed to the atmosphere. Rocks containing iron are often gray when freshly broken away. However, the combination of humidity and oxygen in the atmosphere cause the gray iron to oxidize and become red rust.

Cave system (right)
The fascinating, sculpted objects in this cave have been formed by chemical erosion and deposition.

IT'S A FACT
Rocks erode chemically by dissolution, hydrolysis, and oxidation in varying combinations, because they themselves are usually made from complex minerals. This is evident when looking at a weathered surface because some areas have eroded more quickly than others, depending on their composition.

Rain and wind cycles dictate worldwide weather conditions, determining the redistribution of fresh water over the landmasses. Both are controlled by the flow of energy in the atmosphere as it is the contrast in temperature between atmospheric zones that causes their movement.

FRESH WATER undergoes a distinct cycle. Taking the oceans as the starting point, the first stage in the cycle is evaporation of water vapor from the surface. The energy from the Sun causes warming of the very top layer of the water so that water molecules are released into the air. The same thing happens on land, from wet ground and organisms. Pockets of warm air, carrying the water vapor, then rise through the atmosphere as columns called thermals. This process is called convection. It occurs because the molecules in warm air are more widely spaced than those in cold air, so the warm air is less dense than the cold.

Wet and dry (right)
Owing to a combination of latitude and geography, certain places have higher annual rainfall than others. The first map (right) shows the highest annual global rainfall, while the second (opposite page) concentrates on the lowest figures.

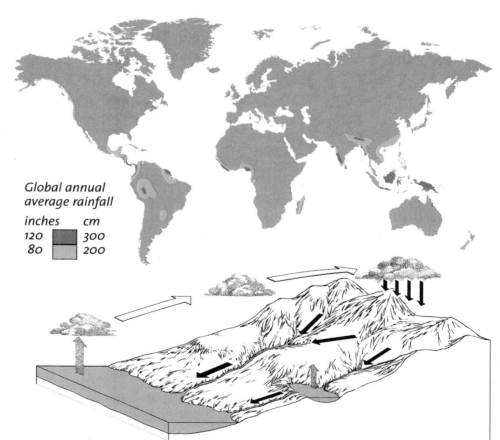

Global annual average rainfall

inches		cm
120		300
80		200

Water cycle (right)
This illustration simplifies the process by which water circulates from the oceans to the land, and then back again to the oceans.

The forces generated by convection culminate in winds, as the atmosphere becomes a swirling mass of cold and warm air currents. Inevitably this means that humid air pockets cool down at high altitude, and can no longer carry their loads of water vapor. The result is that the water vapor is forced to condense with the loss of energy. As it condenses, it becomes visible as clouds. Eventually the clouds' coalescing droplets may form raindrops falling from the sky.

Much rain falls straight back into the oceans to await evaporation once again, but a significant amount falls on land. This rainfall runs off the land and collects into streams and rivers, eventually finding its way back to the oceans.

IT'S A FACT
The energy that the rain and wind cycles depend upon comes from the Sun, as its rays penetrate the atmosphere. Consequently there are notable and predictable changes to the cycles that happen annually, because varying amounts of energy are available in different parts of the world. This means that reasonably reliable maps can be made to forecast seasonal weather patterns on an international scale.

Global annual
average rainfall

inches	cm
20	50
10	25

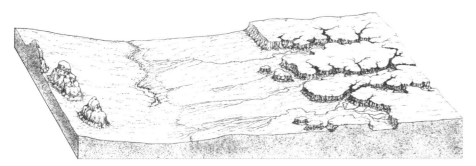

Erosion (left)
Incessant rainwater gradually strips fertile land of its nutrients, which are washed out to sea.

© DIAGRAM

Water is an abundant ingredient of the Earth's atmosphere. The average temperature at the surface of the Earth fluctuates between parameters only slightly above and below the freezing point of water. This means that water can exist in its three fundamental states: solid (ice), liquid (water), and gaseous (vapor).

IN THESE STATES, water is able to act on the other materials that make up the Earth's atmospheric environment by physical or chemical means—usually simultaneously. Hence, the form of the Earth's crust is dictated by two major agents: seismic action from beneath, and water action from above.

Physically, water acts on materials in a number of ways. Since water is not compressible, it can strike at surfaces with great force, and break down materials with the release of kinetic energy. A good example is the action of waves breaking against cliffs.

For the same reason, water is also extremely effective at pushing and carrying materials from

Erosion by exfoliation (below)
In arid regions rock surfaces heat up when exposed to the Sun (top right), and contract as the temperature falls at night (middle right). Over a period of time, surface layers of rock peel off, and fall to the ground (bottom right). The illustration (below) shows a cutaway view of a boulder, or dome, which has been subject to exfoliation.

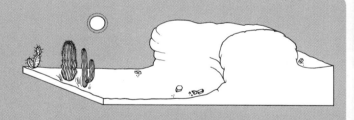

one place to another as it flows. This is seen in stream and river systems, where valleys are created by the transportation of vast quantities of bedrock over time. Of course, many inorganic materials become buoyant or semi-buoyant in water, making it even easier for the water to transport them.

Water also has the capacity to break up materials physically when it has very little stored energy. This is because water expands as it freezes. If the water is absorbed into porous rock, or lying within cracks when it freezes, then it can explode the material into smaller fragments.

Cliff erosion (above)
Cliffs made from chalk are very susceptible to water erosion by a combination of chemical and physical action.

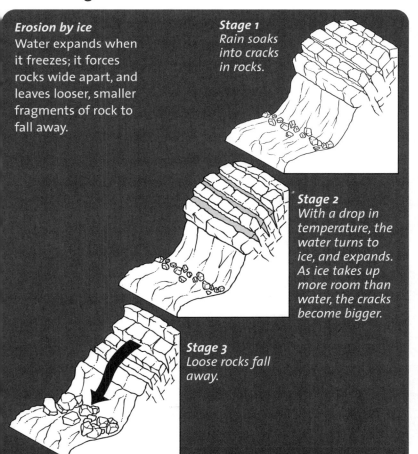

Erosion by ice
Water expands when it freezes; it forces rocks wide apart, and leaves looser, smaller fragments of rock to fall away.

Stage 1
Rain soaks into cracks in rocks.

Stage 2
With a drop in temperature, the water turns to ice, and expands. As ice takes up more room than water, the cracks become bigger.

Stage 3
Loose rocks fall away.

IT'S A FACT
Chemically, water acts as a universal solvent so that rocks may completely or partially dissolve on contact. Others become suspended in water. Unlike those in a solution, the particles in a suspension are not actually dissolved: they are so small they are held between the water molecules. Strictly speaking therefore, a suspension is a physical action on a microscopic scale. Water also assists in the oxidation of some mineral components.

© DIAGRAM

Wind is the translation of solar energy into the movement of air molecules. It occurs as the result of air molecules being warmed by heat radiating from the surface of lands and oceans.

CONVECTION CURRENTS are initiated by ascending thermals, so that hot regions of the atmosphere rise while cold regions descend. This is because warm air molecules are more widely dispersed than cold ones, so that warm air is less dense than cold air. Ultimately, the atmosphere divides invisibly into layers of warm and cold air.

However, these layers cannot stabilize very easily due to the continued convection, the rotation of the Earth, the cycle of night and day, and the temperature variables between the equatorial, temperate, and polar zones of the planet's atmosphere. The result is that huge convective movements occur, which we experience as wind.

Winds are only really effective at moving minute particles, such as dust and sand, which accounts for the existence of

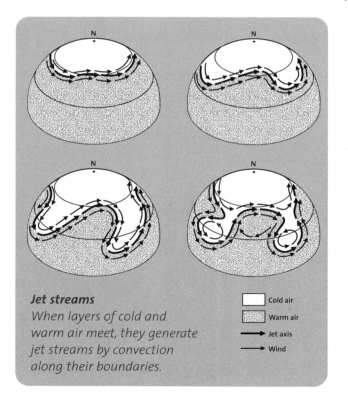

Jet streams
When layers of cold and warm air meet, they generate jet streams by convection along their boundaries.

☐ Cold air
▨ Warm air
→ Jet axis
→ Wind

dust bowls and sandy deserts. This is because air molecules compress together when they blow against larger pieces of rock, failing to gather enough energy to move them.

Winds do most damage in combination with water. This is because the kinetic energy in the wind is absorbed into the water, which is better at acting on materials. This is particularly evident over large bodies of water, such as oceans, seas, and lakes.

When wind blows over the water's surface it translates into wave energy. If the wind is blowing inland, waves then travel toward the shoreline, where the energy is unleashed onto rocks, cliffs, and beaches, causing erosion.

IT'S A FACT
Wind can vary in its speed, and this reflects the amount of kinetic energy it possesses. The English admiral Sir Francis Beaufort (1774–1857) devised his Beaufort scale (forces 0–12) as a means of expressing wind strength. For example, "calm" is force 0—less than 0.6 miles per hour (1 km per hour) and "hurricane" is force 12—65 miles per hour (118 kmph or more).

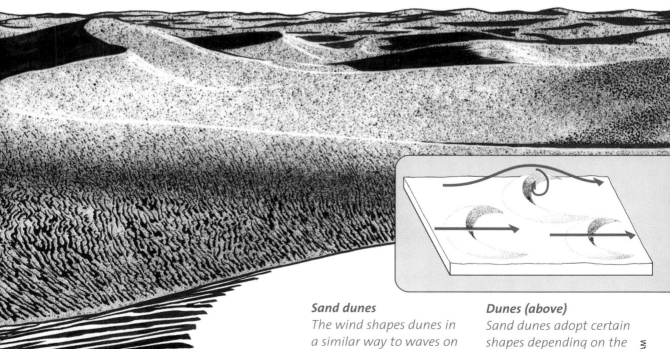

Sand dunes
The wind shapes dunes in a similar way to waves on the surface of an ocean.

Dunes (above)
Sand dunes adopt certain shapes depending on the direction of the wind.

© DIAGRAM

Although ice is commonly called a solid, it is in fact a fluid, but with very high viscosity, or resistance to flow. This helps in understanding the way that ice acts on materials.

IN REGIONS WHERE LOW TEMPERATURES promote the creation of ice, such as the Arctic, Antarctic, and mountain ranges, it often accumulates to form vast ice "rivers" called glaciers. Glaciers are fed by the accumulation of snow, which compresses into ice under its own weight, and then begins to flow downhill due to gravity.

Glaciers behave in similar ways to rivers, but in super-slow motion. Any loose pieces of debris become enveloped by the ice and transported by it. In addition the debris scores the bedrock surface beneath the ice, causing further erosion. In some places erosion features called *roches moutonnées* (rock sheep) demonstrate the direction of flow over ancient glacial landscapes. They have one smoothed and gently sloping face, and a corresponding ragged and steeply-sloping face.

Less dramatic, though no less effective, is the action ice can have on materials as it forms from cooling water. Water expands when it solidifies, so that it can force materials apart if held inside or between cracks in rock. When the freezing process is punctuated by periods of melting, it results in a phenomenon known as freeze–thaw erosion, or ice wedging. This causes whole mountainsides and cliff faces to break up, layer by layer. The separated pieces of rock accumulate in cone-shaped piles and are referred to as talus or scree.

IT'S A FACT
As ice expands on formation, it is buoyant on water. In places where glaciers terminate at oceans, this can mean that icebergs from a glacier carry eroded materials considerable distances out to sea. Although ice is relatively light it can accumulate into thick sheets that are so heavy that they depress the bedrock. This has happened in Greenland, so that the center of the island is actually below sea level. The same is true of Antarctica and Baffin Island, Canada.

Swiss Alps (above)
Many valleys in the Swiss Alps are still being carved from the rock by glaciers as the altitude allows the ice to remain frozen.

Steep sides (below)
Glacial valleys have characteristically steep sides with overhanging valleys.

Glacial valley (below)
A V-shaped river valley (left) became U-shaped when its river froze to become a glacier during the Ice Age (middle). Afterward, the river remained on the valley floor (right).

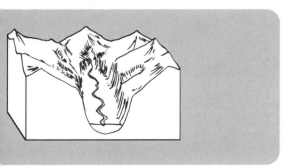

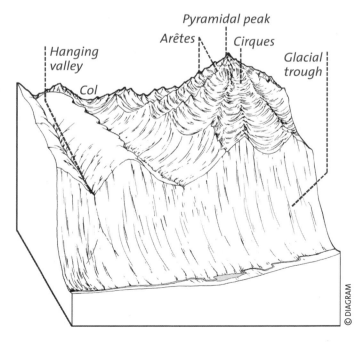

Minerals and soils

Rocks can contain any number of elements and compounds, depending on how and where they were formed. As they comprise different minerals, they have a variety of uses.

SOME ROCKS contain metals and are described as ores. These metals are sometimes in their pure state, such as gold and silver. More often they are chemically combined so that industrial processing is required to extract the metals. Bauxite, for example, is the ore from which aluminum is obtained.

Other rocks are valued for the greater part of their make up. For example, lime (calcium oxide) can be obtained from limestone. When lime is baked with gray clay, the resulting product is

Minerals

Quartz
A compound of silicon and oxygen, it is found in many types of rocks.

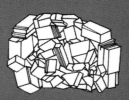

Salt
A compound of sodium and chlorine, it is seawater's most common mineral.

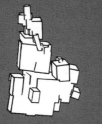

Cassiterite
A compound that includes oxygen and tin, it is the source of the metal tin.

Calcite
Made of calcium, carbon, and oxygen, it is the main mineral in marble and limestone.

Copper mining (above)
The ores that contain copper tend to exist in vast masses rather than in thin layers, which means that opencast mining, rather than shaft mining, is possible.

cement, a material widely used in the construction of buildings, roads, and bridges.

Some types of rock are described as precious stones or gemstones. This is because they comprise concentrations of rare minerals that are valued for their properties. They are the result of rocks being heated so that the substances melt and collect in pockets before crystallizing again. Diamonds are made from carbon, a common element, yet they are highly prized. Corundum is a crystallized form of alumina (Al_2O_3), which is better known in the form of rubies and sapphires.

The nature of rocks before erosion also has a direct influence on the types of soil that result. Loam is a soil consisting of particles of sand and clay, with a certain amount of organic material. Loess is a soil made from windblown deposits. Consequently it comprises a variety of minerals, but the particles are small and loosely compacted. Alluvium is similar to loam, but the organic matter is replaced by silt, an extremely fine blend of mineral grains with a higher surface area to volume ratio, resulting in a fertile soil.

IT'S A FACT
The British crown contains over 400 precious and semi-precious stones set in gold and silver—a reminder of the beauty of the Earth's natural resources.

Iron ore (left)
Iron ore is made from various oxides of iron, so the oxygen needs to be removed to create pure iron.

Gold (right)
Gold is an element that does not react with other chemicals, which means that it is found in its pure, or native, form.

© DIAGRAM

The Moon is integral to the movements of the oceans, which we call tides. This is because the Moon has a gravitational pull that affects the surface of the Earth as it passes overhead.

THE MOON exerts a gravitational pull on the Earth's landmasses, but only oceans move because water is fluid, not solid. The Sun exerts a gravitational pull, too, which also affects the oceans. The result is that the tides operate in a sequence according to the relative positions of the Earth, the Moon, and the Sun.

Each day, coastal regions witness high and low tides twice. Each cycle lasts for about 12 hours and 20 to 25 minutes, so that a shift of 40 to 50 minutes occurs over 24 hours. The tidal range can be considerable—up to several feet (m)—along the coastal regions of large bodies of water. However, in places such as the Mediterranean Sea, the tidal range is only a few inches (cm). When the Sun and Moon are in line with the Earth, there are especially large tidal ranges called spring tides. Small tidal ranges occurring midway between spring tides are called neap tides.

Currents
Wind-driven currents transfer heat around the surface of the oceans (below).

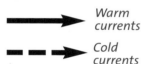

→ Warm currents

⇢ Cold currents

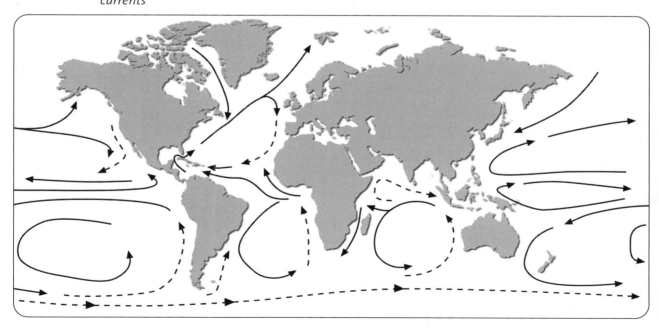

Wind is the main factor driving ocean currents, though the Earth's spin helps to steer them as they circle oceans north and south of the equator in great loops called gyres.

Another reason for currents is the collision of warm and cold waters. Warm water is less dense and tends to rise, while cold water is more dense and tends to sink. The phenomenon is known as convection, and it is prevalent where polar waters meet waters from equatorial regions.

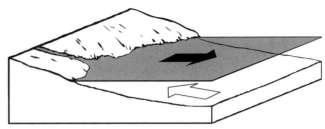

Estuary currents
Where freshwater meets salt water, the contrast in water density produces currents.

Warm and cold water currents
Cold water rises and becomes warm.

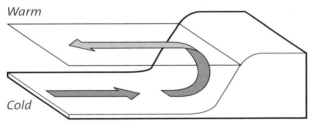

Warm

Cold

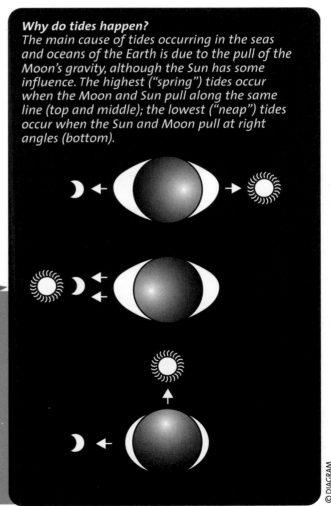

Why do tides happen?
The main cause of tides occurring in the seas and oceans of the Earth is due to the pull of the Moon's gravity, although the Sun has some influence. The highest ("spring") tides occur when the Moon and Sun pull along the same line (top and middle); the lowest ("neap") tides occur when the Sun and Moon pull at right angles (bottom).

IT'S A FACT
A third cause of currents is the meeting of salt water and freshwater in river estuaries. As well as the kinetic energy of the flowing river water, there is a contrast in density between the two types of water. The outcome is similar to convection, so that the freshwater rises over the salt water, causing undercurrents and eddies.

The Earth's surface is subject to seasonal changes because of the planet's varying position as it moves around the Sun over a period of one year. An Earth-year is defined as the length of time it takes for the planet to make a complete orbit of the Sun— 365.3 days.

THE EARTH ORBITS THE SUN in an almost perfect circular path so that its distance from the Sun does not vary enough to cause the changes in temperature we associate with the seasons. However, the axis of the Earth is not perpendicular (90°) to the plane of its orbit. In fact, it is inclined by 23.4°.

As a result, the north is tipped away from the Sun by 23.4° on December 21/22 (midwinter in the Northern Hemisphere, midsummer in the Southern Hemisphere) and is tipped toward the Sun by 23.4° on June 21/22 (midsummer in the Northern Hemisphere, midwinter in the Southern Hemisphere). These times are called the solstices. At the halfway points between the solstices the Earth rotates at 90° to the Sun, so that the Sun is exactly above the equator. These are called the equinoxes. They fall on March 21/22, and September 21/22 approximately.

Temperatures vary through the seasons because the Sun's rays have to travel through different

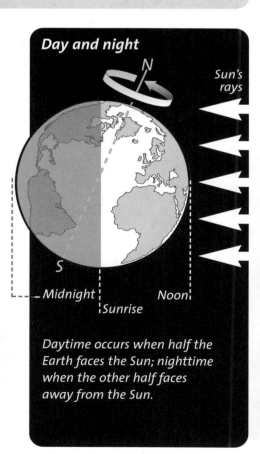

Day and night

N

Sun's rays

S

Midnight ┊ Noon
┊Sunrise

Daytime occurs when half the Earth faces the Sun; nighttime when the other half faces away from the Sun.

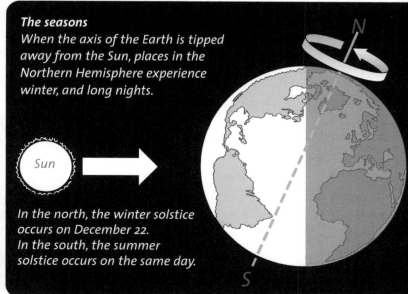

The seasons
When the axis of the Earth is tipped away from the Sun, places in the Northern Hemisphere experience winter, and long nights.

Sun

In the north, the winter solstice occurs on December 22. In the south, the summer solstice occurs on the same day.

N

S

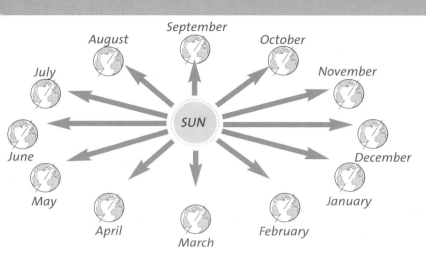

September
August
July
October
November
June
SUN
December
May
January
April
February
March

Monthly positions (right)
The angle of the Earth varies in relation to the position of the Sun during a single orbit, which lasts for one year.

depths of atmosphere—and strike a variable area of the Earth's surface—depending on the angle at which they arrive. In places where the rays meet the Earth's atmosphere at exactly 90°, they have the minimum possible distance to travel to the Earth's surface. Hence, they carry with them the maximum amount of heat energy. This can only occur between the tropics of Cancer and Capricorn.

IT'S A FACT
Elsewhere the rays of the Sun have farther to travel through the atmosphere. There are regions that can witness total darkness over 24 hours in their winter seasons, and 24 hours total light in their summer seasons, such is their angle to the Sun. These are within the Arctic and Antarctic Circles. The regions between the tropics and the polar circles are described as temperate.

© DIAGRAM

N

When the axis of the Earth is angled toward the Sun, places in the Northern Hemisphere experience summer, and short nights.

Sun

In the north, the summer solstice occurs on June 21. In the south, the winter solstice occurs on the same day.

S

The Tropics	
Arctic Circle	66° 30'N
Tropic of Cancer	23° 27'N
Equator	0°
Tropic of Capricorn	23° 27'S
Antarctic Circle	66° 30'S

As well as the annual climatic changes on Earth, known as the seasons, there are more long-term climatic changes. Some are called ice ages, because the overall climate cools so that polar conditions extend farther south and north. "Glaciation" refers to a phase of extreme cold within an ice age.

GLACIATIONS OCCUR in cycles of tens of thousands of years. At the moment, the Earth is between glacial phases, so it is enjoying generally warmer conditions. There have been about twenty relatively recent glaciations in the present ice age, according to geological evidence.

The cause of ice ages is a combination of three major factors relating to the Earth's orbit around the Sun. Their coincidence has been intermittent so that ice ages have occurred sporadically throughout the Earth's prehistory.

First, the axial tilt of the Earth varies, with a 41,000-year cycle. Second, the Earth actually wobbles on its axis over a period of 21,000 years. Third, the orbital path of the Earth oscillates between a near perfect circle and an ellipse every 46,000 years. The result has been a series of severe ice ages, each punctuated by glaciations, depending on the timing of these three factors. The most recent ice age, dominating the Pleistocene

Ice sheets
During the last ice age— known as "The Ice Age"— the polar region extended down over Europe and North America, covering the land with sheets of ice and snow for thousands of years.

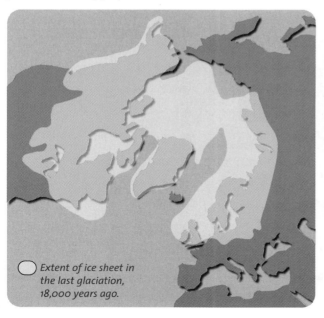

Extent of ice sheet in the last glaciation, 18,000 years ago.

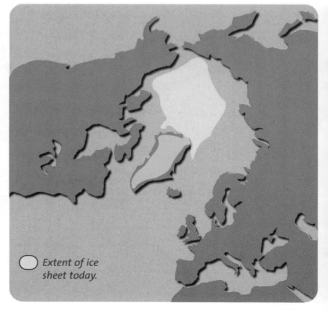

Extent of ice sheet today.

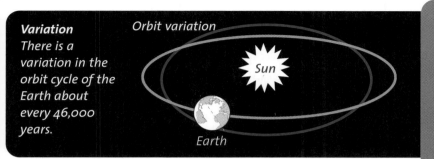

Variation
There is a variation in the orbit cycle of the Earth about every 46,000 years.

Orbit variation

Sun

Earth

Epoch—"The Ice Age," as it is commonly known— was so recent that its effects can still be seen in the landscapes and the organisms of the temperate regions surrounding the poles. This is because those areas were covered by ice sheets and glaciers just like their polar counterparts. In fact, it can be argued that this latest ice age has not yet reached its end properly, so that the Earth will suffer glaciation again within a few thousand years.

IT'S A FACT
The major ice ages are named by scientists and are associated with dates that mark their beginnings and ends. The earliest is called the Huronian, lasting between 2,700 million and 1,800 million years ago. The last one, the Pleistocene Ice Age, started 1.64 million years ago, and may not yet be over!

Mammoths
These hairy elephants were one of the species that evolved to survive in the Northern Hemisphere during the last ice age.

Well-known processes of erosion are responsible for the landscapes we live in. For the most part they have resulted in gentle hills and valleys, but there are some unusual features in certain parts of the world caused by local climate or geology.

MONUMENT VALLEY, in Utah and Arizona, is a spectacular example of a phenomenon known as "differential erosion." This is where separate rock layers, or strata, erode at different rates. The result is that stacks of rock are left standing when erosion has affected the surrounding landscape. The layers of rock on top of each stack, or monument, act like a shield, preventing rainwater from eroding the softer rock beneath it. Bryce Canyon National Park, Utah, has some similar features called columns, which are remarkable for their elegance. Zion National Park, Utah, has the beginnings of a natural arch that is being sculpted by rainwater as it cascades down a cliff face capped with resistant stone.

The features in Utah are all caused by rainwater as it falls and then runs off the landscape. A different form of landscape

Monument Valley
The monuments are rock stacks left by desert weathering and erosion of a plateau.

Fossilized sand dunes
Weathering of the rock above has exposed these remnants of the past.

Arches National Park, Utah
This landscape is also the result of weathering, leaving just a bridge of rock to form an arch.

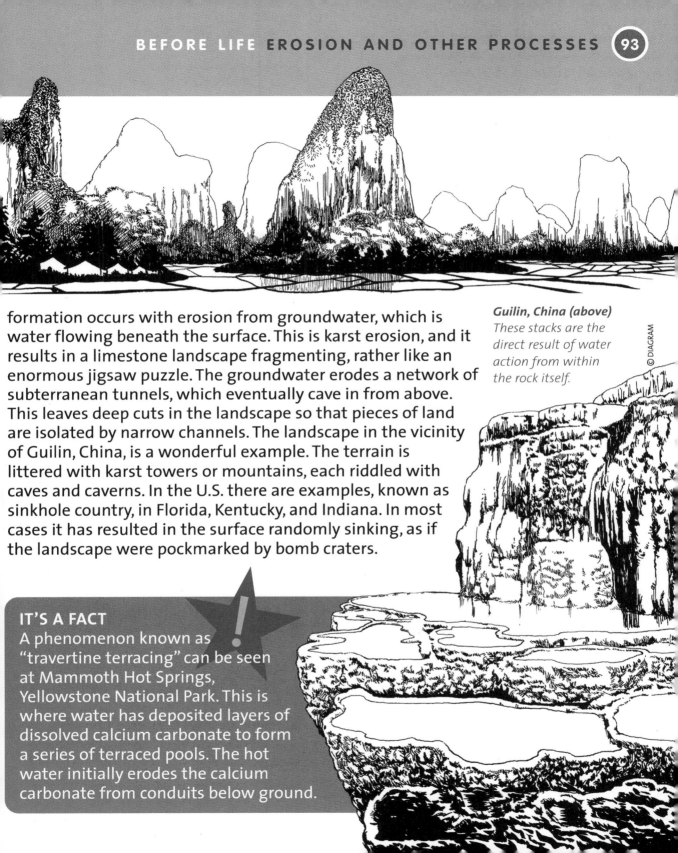

formation occurs with erosion from groundwater, which is water flowing beneath the surface. This is karst erosion, and it results in a limestone landscape fragmenting, rather like an enormous jigsaw puzzle. The groundwater erodes a network of subterranean tunnels, which eventually cave in from above. This leaves deep cuts in the landscape so that pieces of land are isolated by narrow channels. The landscape in the vicinity of Guilin, China, is a wonderful example. The terrain is littered with karst towers or mountains, each riddled with caves and caverns. In the U.S. there are examples, known as sinkhole country, in Florida, Kentucky, and Indiana. In most cases it has resulted in the surface randomly sinking, as if the landscape were pockmarked by bomb craters.

Guilin, China (above)
These stacks are the direct result of water action from within the rock itself.

© DIAGRAM

IT'S A FACT

A phenomenon known as "travertine terracing" can be seen at Mammoth Hot Springs, Yellowstone National Park. This is where water has deposited layers of dissolved calcium carbonate to form a series of terraced pools. The hot water initially erodes the calcium carbonate from conduits below ground.

While the landmasses of the Earth are sculpted by the processes of erosion and seismic activity, the floors of the world's oceans are shaped by deposition and seismic activity.

FOR THE MOST PART, ocean floors are blanketed by thick layers of sediment, but beneath the sediment there are all kinds of interesting features. The sediment is mainly an accumulation of the calcareous remains of single-celled animals called foraminifera. When these are alive, they make up most of the ocean's plankton. The sediment builds up over hundreds of thousands of years to form a gray-white layer called ooze, which can be hundreds of meters thick. The ooze is thickest where the ocean floor is at its most ancient (at subduction zones), and thinnest where the ocean floor is newly generated (along rift lines).

As the oceanic crust is generally much thinner than on land, it is easier to breach by hotspots in the magma layer beneath. Consequently, many ocean floors are littered with submarine volcanoes. In addition, these hotspots tend to remain stationary while the ocean floor continues to move. The result

Beneath the surface
The land beneath the oceans is littered with mountains and valleys.

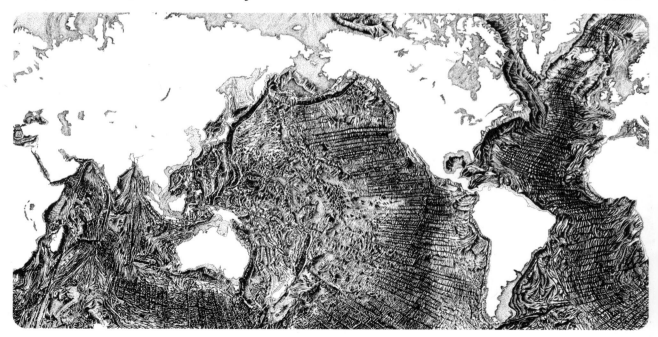

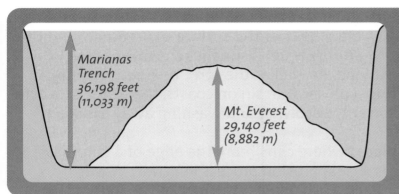

Marianas
Trench
36,198 feet
(11,033 m)

Mt. Everest
29,140 feet
(8,882 m)

IT'S A FACT
The Marianas Trench is located in the western Pacific. At a point called the Challenger Deep the ocean reaches a depth of 36,198 feet (11,033 m)—the greatest depth of any ocean.

is strings of volcanoes marking the progress of the ocean floor. Occasionally, submarine volcanoes manage to break the surface to form volcanic islands. The Pacific Ocean has hundreds of volcanic islands, and many thousands of submarine volcanoes, which are also called seamounts.

Ignoring seamounts and ridges, ocean floors tend to be reasonably flat and level overall. However, traveling toward land, there is typically a steep slope leading up from the abyssal plain (true ocean floor) to a much shallower plateau called the continental shelf. Continental shelves are geologically part of a landmass, rather than part of an ocean floor. They are the result of millions of years of coastal erosion, where the edges of the landmass have been eaten away by wave action to leave a shelflike region, which can be many miles wide.

Topography of the ocean floor

As a result of tectonic processes the ocean floor has developed a variety of features, such as continental crust (a), continental shelf (b), abyssal plain (c), mid-ocean ridge (d), and trench (e).

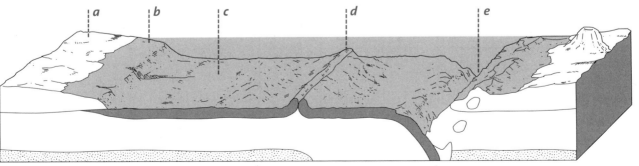

a   b   c   d   e

© DIAGRAM

Coasts are continually subjected to the processes of erosion. Wave action is the primary cause.

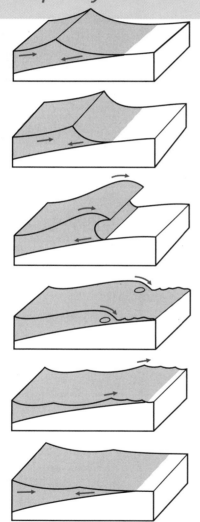

WAVES DERIVE THEIR ENERGY from wind blowing over the surface of an ocean, and this energy is unleashed when waves break against land. As well as the force of kinetic energy exerting a physical strain on coasts, the water also acts as a solvent, dissolving and washing away exposed rock.

In places where cliffs mark the edge of a landmass, there is a clear erosion process in action. Waves continually crash against the rock at the foot of the cliffs, eating the rock away by chemical and physical means. Eventually the waves cut a recess beneath the cliff until the rock above can no longer support its own weight. At this point a section of cliff will fall away into the sea. The waves then pound the remains down until they can once again reach the cliff face, where the process starts all over again. The speed at which the erosion process takes place is dependent on the type of rock comprising the cliffs, and the amount of energy in the waves.

This is clearly demonstrated by differential erosion. When the waves encounter regions of different rock type, they erode them at different rates so that certain coastal features occur. Coves are the result of waves breaking through a wall of resistant rock to reach a region of less resistant rock, with the result that a Ω ("horseshoe") shape is created. If an outcrop of resistant rock exists then the result is a peninsula, where the land has been eroded more quickly on either side—a ΩΩ shape. Ultimately a peninsula will begin to fragment as it erodes. This can result in the formation of stacks and arches as the waves eat the rock away.

Wave action (above)
When ocean waves reach land, friction below causes them to roll over and break on the shore.

Direction of drift

Wind and wave direction

Backwash

Direction of splashing water

IT'S A FACT
In places where rock is insoluble, it is broken down over time into smaller fragments as they rub against one another. Gravel and sand are then transported by the waves along the coast until they reach areas where they build up to form beaches. This process is called "longshore drift."

Differential erosion (below)
Waves usually erode different types of rock at varying rates so that certain coastal features occur. This illustration shows five of these typical features.

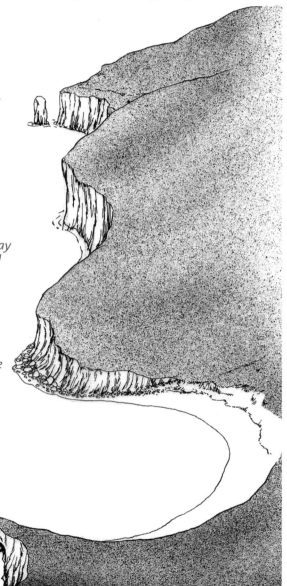

Sea stack—formed when headlands are severely eroded by refracting waves

Steep cliff—formed when waves eat away the rock by chemical and physical means

Boulder beach—a narrow belt of boulders and shingle at the base of a sea cliff

Bay-head beach—a sandy crescent lying in the bay between two rocky promontories

Headland—formed when less resistant rocks are worn away by the sea

Pebbles (left)
Pieces of eroded rock become worn down into smooth round pebbles as wave energy causes them to rub against each other.

© DIAGRAM

It is apparent from the surface of the Moon that space was once filled with asteroids that randomly collided with anything that crossed their flight paths.

THE CRATERS ON THE MOON are millions of years old, but they remain intact because the Moon has no dynamic processes in action to remove them. The story is very different on Earth. Our planet has been struck by foreign bodies with the same frequency as the Moon, but the processes of erosion and seismic activity have removed virtually all traces that this ever happened.

The fact that the Earth has an atmosphere has protected it to some extent. Meteors heat up and burn away with the friction they encounter by passing through the air. However, only the smallest meteors are entirely burned away before reaching the Earth's surface. A great many small meteors do fall on our planet every year. For the most part they go unnoticed, unless they happen to hit a house or car.

In the Earth's prehistory, however, it was colossal meteor strikes that caused some of the fundamental changes to the Earth's living environment.

IT'S A FACT
Scientists have calculated that the Earth was bombarded with asteroids, some as large as 43 miles (64 km) in diameter, until about four billion years ago. Most of the asteroids had collided with something by then, so subsequent collisions happened with less and less frequency. Today, there is little chance of a major strike occurring, but it is inevitable that one will happen eventually.

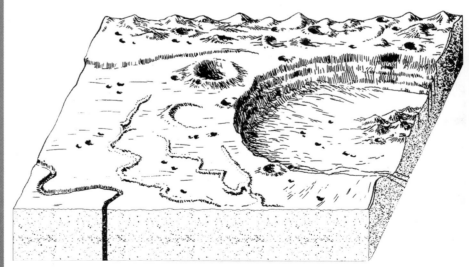

Surface of the Moon
The Moon still displays ancient meteor strike craters because there are no processes of erosion to remove them.

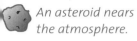
 An asteroid nears the atmosphere.

The asteroid begins to heat up with friction.

Iron meteorite

A particularly large meteor struck the Gulf of Mexico about 65 million years ago, and is regarded by many scientists as the main reason why the dinosaurs became extinct. It would have sent vast amounts of gas, dust, and water vapor into the atmosphere as it plunged into the Earth's crust. This would have blocked the light of the Sun for months, and poisoned the atmosphere, so that many plants and animals could not survive. The crater still exists, but it has been entirely filled by deposits so that it is invisible to the human eye without special surveying equipment.

The burning asteroid is now a meteor.

Stony meteorite

Much of the meteor has vaporized.

The diminished meteor falls to the ground.

The meteor becomes a meteorite.

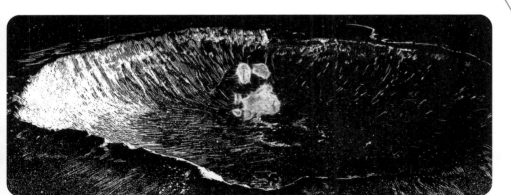

Meteor crater
Meteors explode and vaporize when they collide with the Earth, leaving telltale craters.

© DIAGRAM

When studying the dynamic systems and processes that affect the Earth's surface, it is easy to forget what goes on beneath the ground. We tend to think of landmasses as solid layers of rock, but they are often laced with subterranean channels and cave systems, where groundwater has eroded the land from inside.

I N PLACES WHERE the bedrock is made from soluble minerals, it is often easier for rainwater to soak through the ground and form underground rivers, than to travel over the surface.

Rocks such as chalk and limestone are soluble and permeable. This enables water to enter the rock, and then dissolve it away as it travels. Ultimately the water sculpts channels and caves through the rock. The groundwater may then emerge at the surface, where it encounters a deeper layer of impermeable rock, to form a spring. In some places, the erosion is so extensive that it creates a particular type of landscape called a karst landscape. It is typically marked by depressions and sink holes where the upper layers of the landscape have dropped down due to the collapse of cave roofs.

Caves display certain natural architectural features. They tend to have high vaulted ceilings, where rock has fallen away to form an arch shape. Correspondingly, the floor of a cave is often littered with debris. Water seeping through a cave ceiling will typically be laden with dissolved rock which it precipitates as it drips. The result is the build-up of icicle-like structures which take thousands of years to form. Those which hang from the ceiling are called stalactites, while those on the cave floor are called stalagmites. The reconstituted rock from which they are made is called tufa.

Limestone pavement
In certain places, surface water finds its way through cracks in limestone substrate and begins to dissolve the rock away. Eventually, the cracks open up to leave a "pavement."

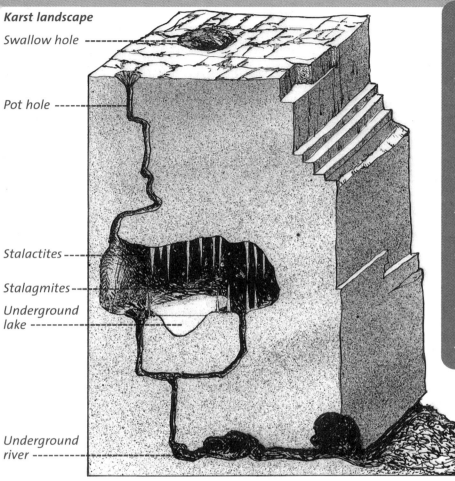

Karst landscape

Swallow hole - - - - - - -

Pot hole - - - - - -

Stalactites - - - - -

Stalagmites - - - - -

Underground lake - - - - - - - - -

Underground river - - - - - - - -

IT'S A FACT

In some places the groundwater becomes trapped between two layers of impermeable rock so that it becomes pressurized. In these circumstances the water will flow upward when a hole is drilled through the upper layer of rock. This is called an artesian well, and requires little or no pumping to force the water to rise to the surface, depending on the natural pressure.

Cave system (left)
Beneath a limestone pavement there is often a complex cave system.

© DIAGRAM

The arrival of life

Early forms of life have been responsible for affecting a large number of geological and geographical features on the Earth.

IT IS DIFFICULT TO CONSIDER the geology and geography of the Earth without acknowledging the responsibility of life-forms for a great many features. For example, certain rock types, such as chalk and limestone, are entirely made from the remains of ancient organisms, yet these rocks cover vast areas. Similarly, atolls are islands made from ancient coral reefs. Crude oil and coal deposits are also derived from the remains of plants and animals. Scientists still cannot say exactly how life began, because they have been unable to reproduce the process in a laboratory. They have, however, managed to devise a process by which the

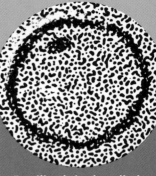

Fossilized single-cell alga
This simple carbon-based life-form lived a billion years ago.

Evolution
Ever since the first primitive organisms appeared on Earth, life has continued to evolve. It will continue to do so as long as the Earth can support life.

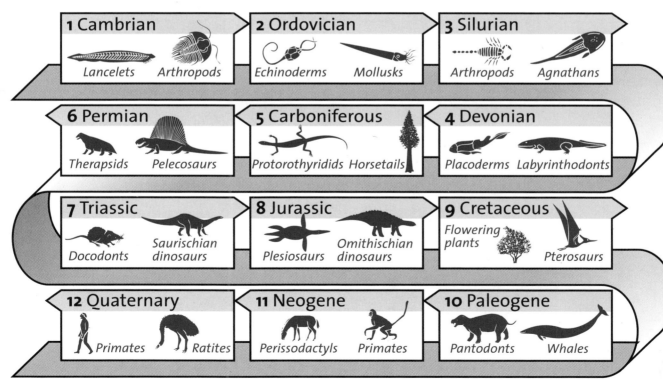

1 Cambrian
Lancelets Arthropods

2 Ordovician
Echinoderms Mollusks

3 Silurian
Arthropods Agnathans

6 Permian
Therapsids Pelecosaurs

5 Carboniferous
Protorothyridids Horsetails

4 Devonian
Placoderms Labyrinthodonts

7 Triassic
Docodonts Saurischian dinosaurs

8 Jurassic
Plesiosaurs Omithischian dinosaurs

9 Cretaceous
Flowering plants Pterosaurs

12 Quaternary
Primates Ratites

11 Neogene
Perissodactyls Primates

10 Paleogene
Pantodonts Whales

IT'S A FACT

We know about past life-forms largely because of the fossil record left inside sedimentary rocks. It is apparent that evolution produced a great many species that are now extinct, but there was a general trend towards species becoming more advanced. Having generated a variety of invertebrate species, natural selection then produced the first vertebrates, and this ultimately led to the evolution of human beings. As long as there is life on planet Earth, the evolutionary story will continue.

fundamental building blocks of life are made. By passing an electric current through a mixture of gases and water they have recreated the conditions once thought to have existed on this planet about 4.3 billion years ago. The experiments have yielded amino acid molecules, from which all life-forms are built using protein molecules. It seems likely that a random process, but on a very large scale and over a very long time, eventually caused the protein molecules to form the simple structures seen in bacteria.

Million years ago

| 7 | 6 | 5 | 4 | 3 | 2 | 1 |

Value	Organism
650	Crustaceans
510	Fish
400	Land plants
370	Insects
350	Seed plants
350	Amphibians
205	Dinosaurs
190	Mammals
150	Birds
140	Flowering plants
4	Humans

The early Earth's carbon dioxide-rich atmosphere would have suffocated any creature now alive. Cyanobacteria (blue-green algae) perhaps transformed this situation. Their chlorophyll used the energy in sunlight to help manufacture food from water and carbon dioxide, releasing oxygen as waste. As breathable amounts of oxygen accumulated in the atmosphere, higher forms of life appeared. First came the protists: single-celled organisms larger than bacteria, and containing a cell nucleus. From certain protists would evolve plants, fungi, and animals.

Evolutionary chart (above)

Not all living forms appeared at the same time. Some have survived millions of years. Others, like humans, are recent arrivals.

© DIAGRAM

Million years ago	Events

15,000–4,500

Universe expanding

Planets forming

15,000 The universe begins by expanding from a central point.
10,000 Vast nebulae separate to begin evolving into galaxies.
9,000 The galaxies become clouds of young stars.
8,000 The stars begin throwing out superfluous material.
7,000 The material begins forming into planets.
6,000 Solar systems complete their formation.
5,000 Planets, moons, asteroids, and comets in orbit.
4,550 Formation of the Earth continues.

Hadean Eon

4,500–4,000

4,500 The Earth and Moon had settled in form.
4,300 An atmosphere forms on the Earth.

Archean Eon

4,000–2,500

Continental crust

4,000 The geology of the Earth begins its formation.
3,500 The first bacterial life-forms appeared on the Earth; five percent of continental crust formed.

Proterozoic Eon

2,500–543

Multicellular animals

2,500 Fifty percent of continental crust formed; first algal plants begin producing oxygen by photosynthesis.
2,000 "Modern" Earth atmosphere reached.
1,400 First multicellular organisms.
570 First multicellular animals using oxygen by respiration.

Phanerozoic Eon

543–now

300 Single landmass (Pangaea) formed.
200 Pangaea breaks into two regions.

Pangaea

Fossils help scientists determine when different kinds of plants and animals first appeared.

Era	Millions of years ago	Period	Main events
Proterozoic Eon	2,500–543	Proterozoic periods	bacteria, simple animals, and plants exist
Paleozoic	543–490	Cambrian	sea animals without a backbone flourish
	490–443	Ordovician	early fish appear
	443–417	Silurian	land plants and land arthropods appear
	417–354	Devonian	insects and amphibians appear
	354–290	Carboniferous	reptiles and flying insects live in forests
	290–248	Permian	reptiles dominate
Mesozoic	248–206	Triassic	dinosaurs dominate, mammals appear
	206–144	Jurassic	birds appear and pterosaurs flourish
	144–65	Cretaceous	flowering plants appear
Cenozoic	65–1.8	Tertiary	dinosaurs die out, mammals spread
	1.8–present	Quaternary	humans dominate

© DIAGRAM

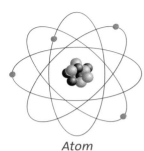

Atom

Chemical erosion

Conglomerate rock

Fossil

antimatter Best explained as the exact opposite of matter, so that an equilibrium or balance exists in the universe. See **matter**.

atmosphere The layer of gases above the surface of a planet or moon, and what we often call the air.

atom One of the identical constituent particles of a chemical element, comprising electrons, protons, and neutrons in a precise arrangement.

boiling point The temperature at which an element or compound possesses enough energy for its atoms or particles to become so agitated that they convert from a liquid to a gas.

cement A hard precipitous material, usually calcium-rich, that fills the spaces between particles of rock and adheres them together.

chemical erosion The wearing-away effects of weathering that alter the chemical composition of rock.

compound A substance or chemical, comprising two or more elements. See **element**, **molecule**.

conglomerate rock A type of aggregate rock, similar to sedimentary rock, but comprising particles of varying rather than uniform size.

continental drift The ongoing movement of the continental landmasses as the result of alterations to the tectonic plates that comprise the Earth's crust, upon which they sit.

convection The movement caused when a low-density substance rises through a higher density material, usually of the same substance but at a lower temperature.

density The relative mass of a substance for a set unit volume of it. See **mass**.

electron A negatively charged, subatomic particle that is part of an atom and orbits the nucleus. See **proton**.

element 1. One of the fundamental chemical substances from which all animals, plants, and minerals are made. 2. One of the factors that make up the weather ("the elements").

erosion The combination of factors—physical and chemical—that break down bedrock until it eventually becomes particles of soil.

evaporation The conversion of atoms or molecules from a liquid to a gas at the surface of a substance due to energy absorption.

fossil Either a mineralized facsimile of an organic object, or a cast of a feature set in mineral.

freezing point The temperature at which an element or compound loses energy so that its atoms or molecules eventually stop moving and it converts from a liquid to a solid.

galaxy A cloud of solar systems and nebulae rotating around a central neutron star, or black hole.

gas The term used to describe an element or compound in its vapor state, so that the atoms or molecules are energized.

gravity The natural force of mutual attraction between all particles of matter, expressed most clearly as the force that makes things fall to the ground, i.e., the attraction between an object and the Earth.

igneous rock A type of crystalline rock originating from the magma beneath the Earth's crust, where it has cooled and solidified.

lava A type of rock formed when magma spews from a volcano and cools too quickly to form crystals.

light-year A unit of distance, not time, defined by how far light travels through space in a single year, i.e., nearly 6,000 billion miles (9,460 billion kilometers).

liquid The term used to describe an element or compound in its fluid state, so that the atoms or molecules are mobile.

magma The name given to the fluid molten rock beneath the Earth's crust, which produces igneous rock when it cools, or lava when it spills from volcanoes.

mass The overall weight of an object, regardless of its density. See **density**.

matter A general term used to describe anything in the universe that is made of atoms. See **antimatter**.

metamorphic rock A type of granular crystalline rock resulting from the compression and heating of sedimentary rocks in which particles have melted and altered in form.

mineral Any solid substance that is not organic by nature, i.e., is inorganic.

mineralization The process by which organic substances are permeated by minerals to become fossils.

molecule A particle comprising the atoms of one, two, or more elements. Compare **compound**.

moon A typically spherical and solid body in orbit around a planet.

mountain A build-up of rock from the Earth's crust between two tectonic plates, where rucking has occurred instead of the creation of a subduction zone. See **volcano**.

nebula A cloud of gas and debris that may evolve into a solar system, or be the remains of a solar system.

neutron A subatomic particle, lacking an electrical charge, and part of the nucleus of an atom.

nucleus 1. The central portion of an atom, comprising neutrons and protons. 2. The central portion of a plant or animal cell, containing the genetic material.

Igneous rock

Lava

Metamorphic rock

Mountain

© DIAGRAM

Physical erosion

Sedimentary rock

Soil

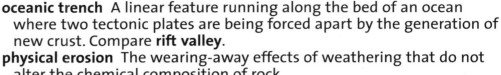

Volcano

oceanic trench A linear feature running along the bed of an ocean where two tectonic plates are being forced apart by the generation of new crust. Compare **rift valley**.

physical erosion The wearing-away effects of weathering that do not alter the chemical composition of rock.

planet Typically a spherical, solid, or gaseous body in orbit around a star.

precipitation 1. The conversion of atoms or molecules from a gas to a liquid state through loss of energy. 2. The deposition of solute from a solution, due to evaporation of the solvent causing saturation. 3. Rain, snow, or hail.

proton A positively charged, subatomic particle that is part of an atom's nucleus. Compare **electron**.

rift valley A linear feature on land resulting from the generation of new crust between two tectonic plates. Compare **oceanic trench**.

sedimentary rock A type of granular rock comprising layers of compressed and mineralized deposits of sediment, originally formed on the bed of a lake or sea.

seismic activity Any gradual or sudden alteration to the composure of the Earth's crust due to movements of the tectonic plates.

soil A substance comprising mineral and organic particles in varying proportions and of varying origin.

solar system A star and its orbiting collection of planets, moons, asteroids, comets, and other satellites.

solid Describes an element or compound in its frozen state, where the atoms or molecules are in a fixed position.

space The void or vacuum that exists between astronomical or cosmic bodies.

star A ball of hydrogen gas generating electromagnetic radiation in the form of light and heat by the reaction of fusion, converting hydrogen into helium.

subduction zone A joint in the Earth's crust where the edge of one tectonic plate is pushed beneath the edge of another.

tectonic plate One of the polygonal sheets of rock that form the surface or crust of the Earth, below the lands and oceans.

volcano A mount or mountain, on land or underwater, made from lava where magma has escaped through the Earth's crust above a pressure point or hotspot. See **mountain**.

weathering The erosive, or wearing away, effect of the weather on substances, including the effects of temperature variation, sunlight, rain, and wind.

There is a lot of useful information on the internet. There are also many sites that are fun to use. Remember that you may be able to get information on a particular topic by using a search engine such as Google (*http://www.google.com*). Some of the sites that are found in this way may be very useful, others not. Below is a selection of websites related to the material covered by this book. Most are illustrated, and they are mainly of the type that provides useful facts.

Facts On File, Inc. *takes no responsibility for the information contained within these websites. All the sites were accessible as of September 1, 2003.*

Astronomy
The home page of **Astronomy** magazine, with links to many sites dealing with the universe, galaxies, stars, and the solar system.
> *http://www.astronomy.com*

Astronomy for Kids
A site for younger students, packed with information, puzzles, and quizzes about the planets.
> *http://www.dustbunny.com/afk/*

British Geological Survey: Education
Includes detailed geological timecharts and scholarly resources.
> *http://www.bgs.ac.uk/education/*

Geology Link Student Resource Center
A look at the geology of the Earth, including reports on current geological activity in the crust.
> *http://www.geologylink.com*

Geological Survey: Learning Web
An educational site exploring the Earth, including rocks and minerals, land, water, and living things. Specifically for K–12 age groups.
> *http://www.usgs.gov/education/*

Liftoff to Space Exploration
A NASA site for teenagers.
> *http://liftoff.msfc.nasa.gov*

National Radio Astronomy Observatory
The National Radio Astronomy Observatory website, with information for both specialists and nonspecialists about telescopes and images of the night sky.
> *http://www.nrao.edu*

Nature
Science news from the online journal.
http://www.nature.com

New Scientist
Online news from the world of science.
http://www.newscientist.com

Open Directory Project: Earthquakes
A comprehensive listing of internet resources.
http://dmoz.org/Science/Earth_Sciences/Geophysics/Earthquakes/

Open Directory Project: Tectonics
A comprehensive listing of internet resources.
http://dmoz.org/Science/Earth_Sciences/Geology/Tectonics/

Scientific American
News from the world of science and technology.
http://www.sciam.com

Solar System Exploration
A NASA site looking at the planets, space exploration, and current scientific theories, evidence, and research about the Earth and its neighbors in the solar system.
http://solarsystem.nasa.gov/features/planets/earth/earth.html

SpaceWeather.com
A look at the interaction of the Sun with the Earth, with details of solar flares, geomagnetic storms, auroras, and electrical storms.
http://www.spaceweather.com

University of Texas, McDonald Observatory: Stardate
A detailed survey of the Earth, including geography, geology, tides, climate, and exploration.
http://stardate.org/resources/ssguide/earth.html

Views of the Solar System
A comprehensive multimedia tour of the Sun, the planets, and other cosmic bodies within the solar system, with statistical data, detailed information, pictures, and videos.
http://www.solarviews.com